C-1923   CAREER EXAMINATION SERIES

This is your
PASSBOOK for...

School Guard (Safety Agent)

Test Preparation Study Guide
Questions & Answers

COPYRIGHT NOTICE

This book is SOLELY intended for, is sold ONLY to, and its use is RESTRICTED to individual, bona fide applicants or candidates who qualify by virtue of having seriously filed applications for appropriate license, certificate, professional and/or promotional advancement, higher school matriculation, scholarship, or other legitimate requirements of education and/or governmental authorities.

This book is NOT intended for use, class instruction, tutoring, training, duplication, copying, reprinting, excerption, or adaptation, etc., by:

1) Other publishers
2) Proprietors and/or Instructors of "Coaching" and/or Preparatory Courses
3) Personnel and/or Training Divisions of commercial, industrial, and governmental organizations
4) Schools, colleges, or universities and/or their departments and staffs, including teachers and other personnel
5) Testing Agencies or Bureaus
6) Study groups which seek by the purchase of a single volume to copy and/or duplicate and/or adapt this material for use by the group as a whole without having purchased individual volumes for each of the members of the group
7) Et al.

Such persons would be in violation of appropriate Federal and State statutes.

PROVISION OF LICENSING AGREEMENTS – Recognized educational, commercial, industrial, and governmental institutions and organizations, and others legitimately engaged in educational pursuits, including training, testing, and measurement activities, may address request for a licensing agreement to the copyright owners, who will determine whether, and under what conditions, including fees and charges, the materials in this book may be used them. In other words, a licensing facility exists for the legitimate use of the material in this book on other than an individual basis. However, it is asseverated and affirmed here that the material in this book CANNOT be used without the receipt of the express permission of such a licensing agreement from the Publishers. Inquiries re licensing should be addressed to the company, attention rights and permissions department.

All rights reserved, including the right of reproduction in whole or in part, in any form or by any means, electronic or mechanical, including photocopying, recording, or by any information storage and retrieval system, without permission in writing from the Publisher.

Copyright © 2024 by
National Learning Corporation

212 Michael Drive, Syosset, NY 11791
(516) 921-8888 • www.passbooks.com
E-mail: info@passbooks.com

PUBLISHED IN THE UNITED STATES OF AMERICA

PASSBOOK® SERIES

THE *PASSBOOK® SERIES* has been created to prepare applicants and candidates for the ultimate academic battlefield – the examination room.

At some time in our lives, each and every one of us may be required to take an examination – for validation, matriculation, admission, qualification, registration, certification, or licensure.

Based on the assumption that every applicant or candidate has met the basic formal educational standards, has taken the required number of courses, and read the necessary texts, the *PASSBOOK® SERIES* furnishes the one special preparation which may assure passing with confidence, instead of failing with insecurity. Examination questions – together with answers – are furnished as the basic vehicle for study so that the mysteries of the examination and its compounding difficulties may be eliminated or diminished by a sure method.

This book is meant to help you pass your examination provided that you qualify and are serious in your objective.

The entire field is reviewed through the huge store of content information which is succinctly presented through a provocative and challenging approach – the question-and-answer method.

A climate of success is established by furnishing the correct answers at the end of each test.

You soon learn to recognize types of questions, forms of questions, and patterns of questioning. You may even begin to anticipate expected outcomes.

You perceive that many questions are repeated or adapted so that you can gain acute insights, which may enable you to score many sure points.

You learn how to confront new questions, or types of questions, and to attack them confidently and work out the correct answers.

You note objectives and emphases, and recognize pitfalls and dangers, so that you may make positive educational adjustments.

Moreover, you are kept fully informed in relation to new concepts, methods, practices, and directions in the field.

You discover that you are actually taking the examination all the time: you are preparing for the examination by "taking" an examination, not by reading extraneous and/or supererogatory textbooks.

In short, this PASSBOOK®, used directedly, should be an important factor in helping you to pass your test.

SCHOOL GUARD (SAFETY AGENT)

DUTIES AND RESPONSIBILITIES

School Guards (Safety Agents), under general supervision, patrol designated areas of school buildings and surrounding areas; identify and prevent infiltration of unlawful or prohibited items through scanning; give routine information to visitors and direct them to the proper personnel and offices; request identification of, and remove from the premises, any unauthorized persons; aid sick and injured persons and call for medical, police or fire assistance, when needed; notify supervisors of all emergency incidents and complete any related documentation; respond to altercations between students and other persons, and attempt to separate the involved persons and resolve conflicts; maintain records of persons entering and leaving buildings; monitor security camera systems to ensure facility entrances are secure; identify persons violating Department of Education Rules and Regulations; apprehend persons violating the Penal Law, notify the proper administrative personnel; prepare reports and testify in regard to these violations at a Superintendent's or Principal's hearing and/or in court; monitor and use radio to request assistance from co-workers; may operate a motor vehicle; and perform related work.

SCOPE OF THE EXAMINATION

The multiple-choice test will cover knowledge, skills and/or abilities in such areas as written comprehension and expression; memorization; problem sensitivity; deductive and inductive reasoning; information ordering; spatial orientation; visualization; and other related areas.

HOW TO TAKE A TEST

I. YOU MUST PASS AN EXAMINATION

A. *WHAT EVERY CANDIDATE SHOULD KNOW*

Examination applicants often ask us for help in preparing for the written test. What can I study in advance? What kinds of questions will be asked? How will the test be given? How will the papers be graded?

As an applicant for a civil service examination, you may be wondering about some of these things. Our purpose here is to suggest effective methods of advance study and to describe civil service examinations.

Your chances for success on this examination can be increased if you know how to prepare. Those "pre-examination jitters" can be reduced if you know what to expect. You can even experience an adventure in good citizenship if you know why civil service exams are given.

B. *WHY ARE CIVIL SERVICE EXAMINATIONS GIVEN?*

Civil service examinations are important to you in two ways. As a citizen, you want public jobs filled by employees who know how to do their work. As a job seeker, you want a fair chance to compete for that job on an equal footing with other candidates. The best-known means of accomplishing this two-fold goal is the competitive examination.

Exams are widely publicized throughout the nation. They may be administered for jobs in federal, state, city, municipal, town or village governments or agencies.

Any citizen may apply, with some limitations, such as the age or residence of applicants. Your experience and education may be reviewed to see whether you meet the requirements for the particular examination. When these requirements exist, they are reasonable and applied consistently to all applicants. Thus, a competitive examination may cause you some uneasiness now, but it is your privilege and safeguard.

C. *HOW ARE CIVIL SERVICE EXAMS DEVELOPED?*

Examinations are carefully written by trained technicians who are specialists in the field known as "psychological measurement," in consultation with recognized authorities in the field of work that the test will cover. These experts recommend the subject matter areas or skills to be tested; only those knowledges or skills important to your success on the job are included. The most reliable books and source materials available are used as references. Together, the experts and technicians judge the difficulty level of the questions.

Test technicians know how to phrase questions so that the problem is clearly stated. Their ethics do not permit "trick" or "catch" questions. Questions may have been tried out on sample groups, or subjected to statistical analysis, to determine their usefulness.

Written tests are often used in combination with performance tests, ratings of training and experience, and oral interviews. All of these measures combine to form the best-known means of finding the right person for the right job.

II. HOW TO PASS THE WRITTEN TEST

A. NATURE OF THE EXAMINATION

To prepare intelligently for civil service examinations, you should know how they differ from school examinations you have taken. In school you were assigned certain definite pages to read or subjects to cover. The examination questions were quite detailed and usually emphasized memory. Civil service exams, on the other hand, try to discover your present ability to perform the duties of a position, plus your potentiality to learn these duties. In other words, a civil service exam attempts to predict how successful you will be. Questions cover such a broad area that they cannot be as minute and detailed as school exam questions.

In the public service similar kinds of work, or positions, are grouped together in one "class." This process is known as *position-classification*. All the positions in a class are paid according to the salary range for that class. One class title covers all of these positions, and they are all tested by the same examination.

B. FOUR BASIC STEPS

1) Study the announcement

How, then, can you know what subjects to study? Our best answer is: "Learn as much as possible about the class of positions for which you've applied." The exam will test the knowledge, skills and abilities needed to do the work.

Your most valuable source of information about the position you want is the official exam announcement. This announcement lists the training and experience qualifications. Check these standards and apply only if you come reasonably close to meeting them.

The brief description of the position in the examination announcement offers some clues to the subjects which will be tested. Think about the job itself. Review the duties in your mind. Can you perform them, or are there some in which you are rusty? Fill in the blank spots in your preparation.

Many jurisdictions preview the written test in the exam announcement by including a section called "Knowledge and Abilities Required," "Scope of the Examination," or some similar heading. Here you will find out specifically what fields will be tested.

2) Review your own background

Once you learn in general what the position is all about, and what you need to know to do the work, ask yourself which subjects you already know fairly well and which need improvement. You may wonder whether to concentrate on improving your strong areas or on building some background in your fields of weakness. When the announcement has specified "some knowledge" or "considerable knowledge," or has used adjectives like "beginning principles of…" or "advanced … methods," you can get a clue as to the number and difficulty of questions to be asked in any given field. More questions, and hence broader coverage, would be included for those subjects which are more important in the work. Now weigh your strengths and weaknesses against the job requirements and prepare accordingly.

3) Determine the level of the position

Another way to tell how intensively you should prepare is to understand the level of the job for which you are applying. Is it the entering level? In other words, is this the position in which beginners in a field of work are hired? Or is it an intermediate or advanced level? Sometimes this is indicated by such words as "Junior" or "Senior" in the class title. Other jurisdictions use Roman numerals to designate the level – Clerk I, Clerk II, for example. The word "Supervisor" sometimes appears in the title. If the level is not indicated by the title, check the description of duties. Will you be working under very close supervision, or will you have responsibility for independent decisions in this work?

4) Choose appropriate study materials

Now that you know the subjects to be examined and the relative amount of each subject to be covered, you can choose suitable study materials. For beginning level jobs, or even advanced ones, if you have a pronounced weakness in some aspect of your training, read a modern, standard textbook in that field. Be sure it is up to date and has general coverage. Such books are normally available at your library, and the librarian will be glad to help you locate one. For entry-level positions, questions of appropriate difficulty are chosen – neither highly advanced questions, nor those too simple. Such questions require careful thought but not advanced training.

If the position for which you are applying is technical or advanced, you will read more advanced, specialized material. If you are already familiar with the basic principles of your field, elementary textbooks would waste your time. Concentrate on advanced textbooks and technical periodicals. Think through the concepts and review difficult problems in your field.

These are all general sources. You can get more ideas on your own initiative, following these leads. For example, training manuals and publications of the government agency which employs workers in your field can be useful, particularly for technical and professional positions. A letter or visit to the government department involved may result in more specific study suggestions, and certainly will provide you with a more definite idea of the exact nature of the position you are seeking.

III. KINDS OF TESTS

Tests are used for purposes other than measuring knowledge and ability to perform specified duties. For some positions, it is equally important to test ability to make adjustments to new situations or to profit from training. In others, basic mental abilities not dependent on information are essential. Questions which test these things may not appear as pertinent to the duties of the position as those which test for knowledge and information. Yet they are often highly important parts of a fair examination. For very general questions, it is almost impossible to help you direct your study efforts. What we can do is to point out some of the more common of these general abilities needed in public service positions and describe some typical questions.

1) General information

Broad, general information has been found useful for predicting job success in some kinds of work. This is tested in a variety of ways, from vocabulary lists to questions about current events. Basic background in some field of work, such as sociology or economics, may be sampled in a group of questions. Often these are principles which have become familiar to most persons through exposure rather than through formal training. It is difficult to advise you how to study for these questions; being alert to the world around you is our best suggestion.

2) Verbal ability

An example of an ability needed in many positions is verbal or language ability. Verbal ability is, in brief, the ability to use and understand words. Vocabulary and grammar tests are typical measures of this ability. Reading comprehension or paragraph interpretation questions are common in many kinds of civil service tests. You are given a paragraph of written material and asked to find its central meaning.

3) Numerical ability

Number skills can be tested by the familiar arithmetic problem, by checking paired lists of numbers to see which are alike and which are different, or by interpreting charts and graphs. In the latter test, a graph may be printed in the test booklet which you are asked to use as the basis for answering questions.

4) Observation

A popular test for law-enforcement positions is the observation test. A picture is shown to you for several minutes, then taken away. Questions about the picture test your ability to observe both details and larger elements.

5) Following directions

In many positions in the public service, the employee must be able to carry out written instructions dependably and accurately. You may be given a chart with several columns, each column listing a variety of information. The questions require you to carry out directions involving the information given in the chart.

6) Skills and aptitudes

Performance tests effectively measure some manual skills and aptitudes. When the skill is one in which you are trained, such as typing or shorthand, you can practice. These tests are often very much like those given in business school or high school courses. For many of the other skills and aptitudes, however, no short-time preparation can be made. Skills and abilities natural to you or that you have developed throughout your lifetime are being tested.

Many of the general questions just described provide all the data needed to answer the questions and ask you to use your reasoning ability to find the answers. Your best preparation for these tests, as well as for tests of facts and ideas, is to be at your physical and mental best. You, no doubt, have your own methods of getting into an exam-taking mood and keeping "in shape." The next section lists some ideas on this subject.

IV. KINDS OF QUESTIONS

Only rarely is the "essay" question, which you answer in narrative form, used in civil service tests. Civil service tests are usually of the short-answer type. Full instructions for answering these questions will be given to you at the examination. But in case this is your first experience with short-answer questions and separate answer sheets, here is what you need to know:

1) Multiple-choice Questions

Most popular of the short-answer questions is the "multiple choice" or "best answer" question. It can be used, for example, to test for factual knowledge, ability to solve problems or judgment in meeting situations found at work.

A multiple-choice question is normally one of three types—
- It can begin with an incomplete statement followed by several possible endings. You are to find the one ending which *best* completes the statement, although some of the others may not be entirely wrong.
- It can also be a complete statement in the form of a question which is answered by choosing one of the statements listed.

- It can be in the form of a problem – again you select the best answer.

Here is an example of a multiple-choice question with a discussion which should give you some clues as to the method for choosing the right answer:

When an employee has a complaint about his assignment, the action which will *best* help him overcome his difficulty is to
    A. discuss his difficulty with his coworkers
    B. take the problem to the head of the organization
    C. take the problem to the person who gave him the assignment
    D. say nothing to anyone about his complaint

In answering this question, you should study each of the choices to find which is best. Consider choice "A" – Certainly an employee may discuss his complaint with fellow employees, but no change or improvement can result, and the complaint remains unresolved. Choice "B" is a poor choice since the head of the organization probably does not know what assignment you have been given, and taking your problem to him is known as "going over the head" of the supervisor. The supervisor, or person who made the assignment, is the person who can clarify it or correct any injustice. Choice "C" is, therefore, correct. To say nothing, as in choice "D," is unwise. Supervisors have and interest in knowing the problems employees are facing, and the employee is seeking a solution to his problem.

2) True/False Questions

The "true/false" or "right/wrong" form of question is sometimes used. Here a complete statement is given. Your job is to decide whether the statement is right or wrong.

SAMPLE: A roaming cell-phone call to a nearby city costs less than a non-roaming call to a distant city.

This statement is wrong, or false, since roaming calls are more expensive.
This is not a complete list of all possible question forms, although most of the others are variations of these common types. You will always get complete directions for answering questions. Be sure you understand *how* to mark your answers – ask questions until you do.

V. RECORDING YOUR ANSWERS

Computer terminals are used more and more today for many different kinds of exams.
For an examination with very few applicants, you may be told to record your answers in the test booklet itself. Separate answer sheets are much more common. If this separate answer sheet is to be scored by machine – and this is often the case – it is highly important that you mark your answers correctly in order to get credit.
An electronic scoring machine is often used in civil service offices because of the speed with which papers can be scored. Machine-scored answer sheets must be marked with a pencil, which will be given to you. This pencil has a high graphite content which responds to the electronic scoring machine. As a matter of fact, stray dots may register as answers, so do not let your pencil rest on the answer sheet while you are pondering the correct answer. Also, if your pencil lead breaks or is otherwise defective, ask for another.

Since the answer sheet will be dropped in a slot in the scoring machine, be careful not to bend the corners or get the paper crumpled.

The answer sheet normally has five vertical columns of numbers, with 30 numbers to a column. These numbers correspond to the question numbers in your test booklet. After each number, going across the page are four or five pairs of dotted lines. These short dotted lines have small letters or numbers above them. The first two pairs may also have a "T" or "F" above the letters. This indicates that the first two pairs only are to be used if the questions are of the true-false type. If the questions are multiple choice, disregard the "T" and "F" and pay attention only to the small letters or numbers.

Answer your questions in the manner of the sample that follows:

32. The largest city in the United States is
    A. Washington, D.C.
    B. New York City
    C. Chicago
    D. Detroit
    E. San Francisco

1) Choose the answer you think is best. (New York City is the largest, so "B" is correct.)
2) Find the row of dotted lines numbered the same as the question you are answering. (Find row number 32)
3) Find the pair of dotted lines corresponding to the answer. (Find the pair of lines under the mark "B.")
4) Make a solid black mark between the dotted lines.

VI. BEFORE THE TEST

Common sense will help you find procedures to follow to get ready for an examination. Too many of us, however, overlook these sensible measures. Indeed, nervousness and fatigue have been found to be the most serious reasons why applicants fail to do their best on civil service tests. Here is a list of reminders:

- Begin your preparation early – Don't wait until the last minute to go scurrying around for books and materials or to find out what the position is all about.
- Prepare continuously – An hour a night for a week is better than an all-night cram session. This has been definitely established. What is more, a night a week for a month will return better dividends than crowding your study into a shorter period of time.
- Locate the place of the exam – You have been sent a notice telling you when and where to report for the examination. If the location is in a different town or otherwise unfamiliar to you, it would be well to inquire the best route and learn something about the building.
- Relax the night before the test – Allow your mind to rest. Do not study at all that night. Plan some mild recreation or diversion; then go to bed early and get a good night's sleep.
- Get up early enough to make a leisurely trip to the place for the test – This way unforeseen events, traffic snarls, unfamiliar buildings, etc. will not upset you.
- Dress comfortably – A written test is not a fashion show. You will be known by number and not by name, so wear something comfortable.

- Leave excess paraphernalia at home – Shopping bags and odd bundles will get in your way. You need bring only the items mentioned in the official notice you received; usually everything you need is provided. Do not bring reference books to the exam. They will only confuse those last minutes and be taken away from you when in the test room.
- Arrive somewhat ahead of time – If because of transportation schedules you must get there very early, bring a newspaper or magazine to take your mind off yourself while waiting.
- Locate the examination room – When you have found the proper room, you will be directed to the seat or part of the room where you will sit. Sometimes you are given a sheet of instructions to read while you are waiting. Do not fill out any forms until you are told to do so; just read them and be prepared.
- Relax and prepare to listen to the instructions
- If you have any physical problem that may keep you from doing your best, be sure to tell the test administrator. If you are sick or in poor health, you really cannot do your best on the exam. You can come back and take the test some other time.

VII. AT THE TEST

The day of the test is here and you have the test booklet in your hand. The temptation to get going is very strong. Caution! There is more to success than knowing the right answers. You must know how to identify your papers and understand variations in the type of short-answer question used in this particular examination. Follow these suggestions for maximum results from your efforts:

1) Cooperate with the monitor
The test administrator has a duty to create a situation in which you can be as much at ease as possible. He will give instructions, tell you when to begin, check to see that you are marking your answer sheet correctly, and so on. He is not there to guard you, although he will see that your competitors do not take unfair advantage. He wants to help you do your best.

2) Listen to all instructions
Don't jump the gun! Wait until you understand all directions. In most civil service tests you get more time than you need to answer the questions. So don't be in a hurry. Read each word of instructions until you clearly understand the meaning. Study the examples, listen to all announcements and follow directions. Ask questions if you do not understand what to do.

3) Identify your papers
Civil service exams are usually identified by number only. You will be assigned a number; you must not put your name on your test papers. Be sure to copy your number correctly. Since more than one exam may be given, copy your exact examination title.

4) Plan your time
Unless you are told that a test is a "speed" or "rate of work" test, speed itself is usually not important. Time enough to answer all the questions will be provided, but this does not mean that you have all day. An overall time limit has been set. Divide the total time (in minutes) by the number of questions to determine the approximate time you have for each question.

5) Do not linger over difficult questions

If you come across a difficult question, mark it with a paper clip (useful to have along) and come back to it when you have been through the booklet. One caution if you do this – be sure to skip a number on your answer sheet as well. Check often to be sure that you have not lost your place and that you are marking in the row numbered the same as the question you are answering.

6) Read the questions

Be sure you know what the question asks! Many capable people are unsuccessful because they failed to *read* the questions correctly.

7) Answer all questions

Unless you have been instructed that a penalty will be deducted for incorrect answers, it is better to guess than to omit a question.

8) Speed tests

It is often better NOT to guess on speed tests. It has been found that on timed tests people are tempted to spend the last few seconds before time is called in marking answers at random – without even reading them – in the hope of picking up a few extra points. To discourage this practice, the instructions may warn you that your score will be "corrected" for guessing. That is, a penalty will be applied. The incorrect answers will be deducted from the correct ones, or some other penalty formula will be used.

9) Review your answers

If you finish before time is called, go back to the questions you guessed or omitted to give them further thought. Review other answers if you have time.

10) Return your test materials

If you are ready to leave before others have finished or time is called, take ALL your materials to the monitor and leave quietly. Never take any test material with you. The monitor can discover whose papers are not complete, and taking a test booklet may be grounds for disqualification.

VIII. EXAMINATION TECHNIQUES

1) Read the general instructions carefully. These are usually printed on the first page of the exam booklet. As a rule, these instructions refer to the timing of the examination; the fact that you should not start work until the signal and must stop work at a signal, etc. If there are any *special* instructions, such as a choice of questions to be answered, make sure that you note this instruction carefully.

2) When you are ready to start work on the examination, that is as soon as the signal has been given, read the instructions to each question booklet, underline any key words or phrases, such as *least, best, outline, describe* and the like. In this way you will tend to answer as requested rather than discover on reviewing your paper that you *listed without describing*, that you selected the *worst* choice rather than the *best* choice, etc.

3) If the examination is of the objective or multiple-choice type – that is, each question will also give a series of possible answers: A, B, C or D, and you are called upon to select the best answer and write the letter next to that answer on your answer paper – it is advisable to start answering each question in turn. There may be anywhere from 50 to 100 such questions in the three or four hours allotted and you can see how much time would be taken if you read through all the questions before beginning to answer any. Furthermore, if you come across a question or group of questions which you know would be difficult to answer, it would undoubtedly affect your handling of all the other questions.

4) If the examination is of the essay type and contains but a few questions, it is a moot point as to whether you should read all the questions before starting to answer any one. Of course, if you are given a choice – say five out of seven and the like – then it is essential to read all the questions so you can eliminate the two that are most difficult. If, however, you are asked to answer all the questions, there may be danger in trying to answer the easiest one first because you may find that you will spend too much time on it. The best technique is to answer the first question, then proceed to the second, etc.

5) Time your answers. Before the exam begins, write down the time it started, then add the time allowed for the examination and write down the time it must be completed, then divide the time available somewhat as follows:
    - If 3-1/2 hours are allowed, that would be 210 minutes. If you have 80 objective-type questions, that would be an average of 2-1/2 minutes per question. Allow yourself no more than 2 minutes per question, or a total of 160 minutes, which will permit about 50 minutes to review.
    - If for the time allotment of 210 minutes there are 7 essay questions to answer, that would average about 30 minutes a question. Give yourself only 25 minutes per question so that you have about 35 minutes to review.

6) The most important instruction is to *read each question* and make sure you know what is wanted. The second most important instruction is to *time yourself properly* so that you answer every question. The third most important instruction is to *answer every question*. Guess if you have to but include something for each question. Remember that you will receive no credit for a blank and will probably receive some credit if you write something in answer to an essay question. If you guess a letter – say "B" for a multiple-choice question – you may have guessed right. If you leave a blank as an answer to a multiple-choice question, the examiners may respect your feelings but it will not add a point to your score. Some exams may penalize you for wrong answers, so in such cases *only*, you may not want to guess unless you have some basis for your answer.

7) Suggestions
    a. Objective-type questions
        1. Examine the question booklet for proper sequence of pages and questions
        2. Read all instructions carefully
        3. Skip any question which seems too difficult; return to it after all other questions have been answered
        4. Apportion your time properly; do not spend too much time on any single question or group of questions

5. Note and underline key words – *all, most, fewest, least, best, worst, same, opposite,* etc.
6. Pay particular attention to negatives
7. Note unusual option, e.g., unduly long, short, complex, different or similar in content to the body of the question
8. Observe the use of "hedging" words – *probably, may, most likely,* etc.
9. Make sure that your answer is put next to the same number as the question
10. Do not second-guess unless you have good reason to believe the second answer is definitely more correct
11. Cross out original answer if you decide another answer is more accurate; do not erase until you are ready to hand your paper in
12. Answer all questions; guess unless instructed otherwise
13. Leave time for review

b. Essay questions
1. Read each question carefully
2. Determine exactly what is wanted. Underline key words or phrases.
3. Decide on outline or paragraph answer
4. Include many different points and elements unless asked to develop any one or two points or elements
5. Show impartiality by giving pros and cons unless directed to select one side only
6. Make and write down any assumptions you find necessary to answer the questions
7. Watch your English, grammar, punctuation and choice of words
8. Time your answers; don't crowd material

8) Answering the essay question

Most essay questions can be answered by framing the specific response around several key words or ideas. Here are a few such key words or ideas:

M's: manpower, materials, methods, money, management
P's: purpose, program, policy, plan, procedure, practice, problems, pitfalls, personnel, public relations

a. Six basic steps in handling problems:
1. Preliminary plan and background development
2. Collect information, data and facts
3. Analyze and interpret information, data and facts
4. Analyze and develop solutions as well as make recommendations
5. Prepare report and sell recommendations
6. Install recommendations and follow up effectiveness

b. Pitfalls to avoid
1. *Taking things for granted* – A statement of the situation does not necessarily imply that each of the elements is necessarily true; for example, a complaint may be invalid and biased so that all that can be taken for granted is that a complaint has been registered

2. *Considering only one side of a situation* – Wherever possible, indicate several alternatives and then point out the reasons you selected the best one
3. *Failing to indicate follow up* – Whenever your answer indicates action on your part, make certain that you will take proper follow-up action to see how successful your recommendations, procedures or actions turn out to be
4. *Taking too long in answering any single question* – Remember to time your answers properly

IX. AFTER THE TEST

Scoring procedures differ in detail among civil service jurisdictions although the general principles are the same. Whether the papers are hand-scored or graded by machine we have described, they are nearly always graded by number. That is, the person who marks the paper knows only the number – never the name – of the applicant. Not until all the papers have been graded will they be matched with names. If other tests, such as training and experience or oral interview ratings have been given, scores will be combined. Different parts of the examination usually have different weights. For example, the written test might count 60 percent of the final grade, and a rating of training and experience 40 percent. In many jurisdictions, veterans will have a certain number of points added to their grades.

After the final grade has been determined, the names are placed in grade order and an eligible list is established. There are various methods for resolving ties between those who get the same final grade – probably the most common is to place first the name of the person whose application was received first. Job offers are made from the eligible list in the order the names appear on it. You will be notified of your grade and your rank as soon as all these computations have been made. This will be done as rapidly as possible.

People who are found to meet the requirements in the announcement are called "eligibles." Their names are put on a list of eligible candidates. An eligible's chances of getting a job depend on how high he stands on this list and how fast agencies are filling jobs from the list.

When a job is to be filled from a list of eligibles, the agency asks for the names of people on the list of eligibles for that job. When the civil service commission receives this request, it sends to the agency the names of the three people highest on this list. Or, if the job to be filled has specialized requirements, the office sends the agency the names of the top three persons who meet these requirements from the general list.

The appointing officer makes a choice from among the three people whose names were sent to him. If the selected person accepts the appointment, the names of the others are put back on the list to be considered for future openings.

That is the rule in hiring from all kinds of eligible lists, whether they are for typist, carpenter, chemist, or something else. For every vacancy, the appointing officer has his choice of any one of the top three eligibles on the list. This explains why the person whose name is on top of the list sometimes does not get an appointment when some of the persons lower on the list do. If the appointing officer chooses the second or third eligible, the No. 1 eligible does not get a job at once, but stays on the list until he is appointed or the list is terminated.

X. HOW TO PASS THE INTERVIEW TEST

The examination for which you applied requires an oral interview test. You have already taken the written test and you are now being called for the interview test – the final part of the formal examination.

You may think that it is not possible to prepare for an interview test and that there are no procedures to follow during an interview. Our purpose is to point out some things you can do in advance that will help you and some good rules to follow and pitfalls to avoid while you are being interviewed.

What is an interview supposed to test?

The written examination is designed to test the technical knowledge and competence of the candidate; the oral is designed to evaluate intangible qualities, not readily measured otherwise, and to establish a list showing the relative fitness of each candidate – as measured against his competitors – for the position sought. Scoring is not on the basis of "right" and "wrong," but on a sliding scale of values ranging from "not passable" to "outstanding." As a matter of fact, it is possible to achieve a relatively low score without a single "incorrect" answer because of evident weakness in the qualities being measured.

Occasionally, an examination may consist entirely of an oral test – either an individual or a group oral. In such cases, information is sought concerning the technical knowledges and abilities of the candidate, since there has been no written examination for this purpose. More commonly, however, an oral test is used to supplement a written examination.

Who conducts interviews?

The composition of oral boards varies among different jurisdictions. In nearly all, a representative of the personnel department serves as chairman. One of the members of the board may be a representative of the department in which the candidate would work. In some cases, "outside experts" are used, and, frequently, a businessman or some other representative of the general public is asked to serve. Labor and management or other special groups may be represented. The aim is to secure the services of experts in the appropriate field.

However the board is composed, it is a good idea (and not at all improper or unethical) to ascertain in advance of the interview who the members are and what groups they represent. When you are introduced to them, you will have some idea of their backgrounds and interests, and at least you will not stutter and stammer over their names.

What should be done before the interview?

While knowledge about the board members is useful and takes some of the surprise element out of the interview, there is other preparation which is more substantive. It *is* possible to prepare for an oral interview – in several ways:

1) Keep a copy of your application and review it carefully before the interview

This may be the only document before the oral board, and the starting point of the interview. Know what education and experience you have listed there, and the sequence and dates of all of it. Sometimes the board will ask you to review the highlights of your experience for them; you should not have to hem and haw doing it.

2) Study the class specification and the examination announcement

Usually, the oral board has one or both of these to guide them. The qualities, characteristics or knowledges required by the position sought are stated in these documents. They offer valuable clues as to the nature of the oral interview. For example, if the job involves supervisory responsibilities, the announcement will usually indicate that knowledge of modern supervisory methods and the qualifications of the candidate as a supervisor will be tested. If so, you can expect such questions, frequently in the form of a hypothetical situation which you are expected to solve. NEVER go into an oral without knowledge of the duties and responsibilities of the job you seek.

3) Think through each qualification required

Try to visualize the kind of questions you would ask if you were a board member. How well could you answer them? Try especially to appraise your own knowledge and background in each area, *measured against the job sought*, and identify any areas in which you are weak. Be critical and realistic – do not flatter yourself.

4) Do some general reading in areas in which you feel you may be weak

For example, if the job involves supervision and your past experience has NOT, some general reading in supervisory methods and practices, particularly in the field of human relations, might be useful. Do NOT study agency procedures or detailed manuals. The oral board will be testing your understanding and capacity, not your memory.

5) Get a good night's sleep and watch your general health and mental attitude

You will want a clear head at the interview. Take care of a cold or any other minor ailment, and of course, no hangovers.

What should be done on the day of the interview?

Now comes the day of the interview itself. Give yourself plenty of time to get there. Plan to arrive somewhat ahead of the scheduled time, particularly if your appointment is in the fore part of the day. If a previous candidate fails to appear, the board might be ready for you a bit early. By early afternoon an oral board is almost invariably behind schedule if there are many candidates, and you may have to wait. Take along a book or magazine to read, or your application to review, but leave any extraneous material in the waiting room when you go in for your interview. In any event, relax and compose yourself.

The matter of dress is important. The board is forming impressions about you – from your experience, your manners, your attitude, and your appearance. Give your personal appearance careful attention. Dress your best, but not your flashiest. Choose conservative, appropriate clothing, and be sure it is immaculate. This is a business interview, and your appearance should indicate that you regard it as such. Besides, being well groomed and properly dressed will help boost your confidence.

Sooner or later, someone will call your name and escort you into the interview room. *This is it.* From here on you are on your own. It is too late for any more preparation. But remember, you asked for this opportunity to prove your fitness, and you are here because your request was granted.

What happens when you go in?

The usual sequence of events will be as follows: The clerk (who is often the board stenographer) will introduce you to the chairman of the oral board, who will introduce you to the other members of the board. Acknowledge the introductions before you sit down. Do not be surprised if you find a microphone facing you or a stenotypist sitting by. Oral interviews are usually recorded in the event of an appeal or other review.

Usually the chairman of the board will open the interview by reviewing the highlights of your education and work experience from your application – primarily for the benefit of the other members of the board, as well as to get the material into the record. Do not interrupt or comment unless there is an error or significant misinterpretation; if that is the case, do not hesitate. But do not quibble about insignificant matters. Also, he will usually ask you some question about your education, experience or your present job – partly to get you to start talking and to establish the interviewing "rapport." He may start the actual questioning, or turn it over to one of the other members. Frequently, each member undertakes the questioning on a particular area, one in which he is perhaps most competent, so you can expect each member to participate in the examination. Because time is limited, you may also expect some rather abrupt switches in the direction the questioning takes, so do not be upset by it. Normally, a board member will not pursue a single line of questioning unless he discovers a particular strength or weakness.

After each member has participated, the chairman will usually ask whether any member has any further questions, then will ask you if you have anything you wish to add. Unless you are expecting this question, it may floor you. Worse, it may start you off on an extended, extemporaneous speech. The board is not usually seeking more information. The question is principally to offer you a last opportunity to present further qualifications or to indicate that you have nothing to add. So, if you feel that a significant qualification or characteristic has been overlooked, it is proper to point it out in a sentence or so. Do not compliment the board on the thoroughness of their examination – they have been sketchy, and you know it. If you wish, merely say, "No thank you, I have nothing further to add." This is a point where you can "talk yourself out" of a good impression or fail to present an important bit of information. Remember, *you close the interview yourself.*

The chairman will then say, "That is all, Mr. _____, thank you." Do not be startled; the interview is over, and quicker than you think. Thank him, gather your belongings and take your leave. Save your sigh of relief for the other side of the door.

How to put your best foot forward

Throughout this entire process, you may feel that the board individually and collectively is trying to pierce your defenses, seek out your hidden weaknesses and embarrass and confuse you. Actually, this is not true. They are obliged to make an appraisal of your qualifications for the job you are seeking, and they want to see you in your best light. Remember, they must interview all candidates and a non-cooperative candidate may become a failure in spite of their best efforts to bring out his qualifications. Here are 15 suggestions that will help you:

1) Be natural – Keep your attitude confident, not cocky

If you are not confident that you can do the job, do not expect the board to be. Do not apologize for your weaknesses, try to bring out your strong points. The board is interested in a positive, not negative, presentation. Cockiness will antagonize any board member and make him wonder if you are covering up a weakness by a false show of strength.

2) Get comfortable, but don't lounge or sprawl

Sit erectly but not stiffly. A careless posture may lead the board to conclude that you are careless in other things, or at least that you are not impressed by the importance of the occasion. Either conclusion is natural, even if incorrect. Do not fuss with your clothing, a pencil or an ashtray. Your hands may occasionally be useful to emphasize a point; do not let them become a point of distraction.

3) Do not wisecrack or make small talk

This is a serious situation, and your attitude should show that you consider it as such. Further, the time of the board is limited – they do not want to waste it, and neither should you.

4) Do not exaggerate your experience or abilities

In the first place, from information in the application or other interviews and sources, the board may know more about you than you think. Secondly, you probably will not get away with it. An experienced board is rather adept at spotting such a situation, so do not take the chance.

5) If you know a board member, do not make a point of it, yet do not hide it

Certainly you are not fooling him, and probably not the other members of the board. Do not try to take advantage of your acquaintanceship – it will probably do you little good.

6) Do not dominate the interview

Let the board do that. They will give you the clues – do not assume that you have to do all the talking. Realize that the board has a number of questions to ask you, and do not try to take up all the interview time by showing off your extensive knowledge of the answer to the first one.

7) Be attentive

You only have 20 minutes or so, and you should keep your attention at its sharpest throughout. When a member is addressing a problem or question to you, give him your undivided attention. Address your reply principally to him, but do not exclude the other board members.

8) Do not interrupt

A board member may be stating a problem for you to analyze. He will ask you a question when the time comes. Let him state the problem, and wait for the question.

9) Make sure you understand the question

Do not try to answer until you are sure what the question is. If it is not clear, restate it in your own words or ask the board member to clarify it for you. However, do not haggle about minor elements.

10) Reply promptly but not hastily

A common entry on oral board rating sheets is "candidate responded readily," or "candidate hesitated in replies." Respond as promptly and quickly as you can, but do not jump to a hasty, ill-considered answer.

11) Do not be peremptory in your answers

A brief answer is proper – but do not fire your answer back. That is a losing game from your point of view. The board member can probably ask questions much faster than you can answer them.

12) Do not try to create the answer you think the board member wants

He is interested in what kind of mind you have and how it works – not in playing games. Furthermore, he can usually spot this practice and will actually grade you down on it.

13) Do not switch sides in your reply merely to agree with a board member

Frequently, a member will take a contrary position merely to draw you out and to see if you are willing and able to defend your point of view. Do not start a debate, yet do not surrender a good position. If a position is worth taking, it is worth defending.

14) Do not be afraid to admit an error in judgment if you are shown to be wrong

The board knows that you are forced to reply without any opportunity for careful consideration. Your answer may be demonstrably wrong. If so, admit it and get on with the interview.

15) Do not dwell at length on your present job

The opening question may relate to your present assignment. Answer the question but do not go into an extended discussion. You are being examined for a *new* job, not your present one. As a matter of fact, try to phrase ALL your answers in terms of the job for which you are being examined.

Basis of Rating

Probably you will forget most of these "do's" and "don'ts" when you walk into the oral interview room. Even remembering them all will not ensure you a passing grade. Perhaps you did not have the qualifications in the first place. But remembering them will help you to put your best foot forward, without treading on the toes of the board members.

Rumor and popular opinion to the contrary notwithstanding, an oral board wants you to make the best appearance possible. They know you are under pressure – but they also want to see how you respond to it as a guide to what your reaction would be under the pressures of the job you seek. They will be influenced by the degree of poise you display, the personal traits you show and the manner in which you respond.

ABOUT THIS BOOK

This book contains tests divided into Examination Sections. Go through each test, answering every question in the margin. We have also attached a sample answer sheet at the back of the book that can be removed and used. At the end of each test look at the answer key and check your answers. On the ones you got wrong, look at the right answer choice and learn. Do not fill in the answers first. Do not memorize the questions and answers, but understand the answer and principles involved. On your test, the questions will likely be different from the samples. Questions are changed and new ones added. If you understand these past questions you should have success with any changes that arise. Tests may consist of several types of questions. We have additional books on each subject should more study be advisable or necessary for you. Finally, the more you study, the better prepared you will be. This book is intended to be the last thing you study before you walk into the examination room. Prior study of relevant texts is also recommended. NLC publishes some of these in our Fundamental Series. Knowledge and good sense are important factors in passing your exam. Good luck also helps. So now study this Passbook, absorb the material contained within and take that knowledge into the examination. Then do your best to pass that exam.

EXAMINATION SECTION

EXAMINATION SECTION
TEST 1

DIRECTIONS: Each question or incomplete statement is followed by several suggested answers or completions. Select the one that BEST answers the question or completes the statement. *PRINT THE LETTER OF THE CORRECT ANSWER IN THE SPACE AT THE RIGHT.*

1. Of the following, the MOST important single factor in any building security program is   1.____

    A. a fool-proof employee identification system
    B. an effective control of entrances and exits
    C. bright illumination of all outside areas
    D. clearly marking public and non-public areas

2. There is general agreement that the BEST criterion of what is a good physical security system in a large public building is   2.____

    A. the number of uniformed officers needed to patrol sensitive areas
    B. how successfully the system prevents rather than detects violations
    C. the number of persons caught in the act of committing criminal offenses
    D. how successfully the system succeeds in maintaining good public relations

3. Which one of the following statements most correctly expresses the CHIEF reason why women were originally made eligible for appointment to the position of officer?   3.____

    A. Certain tasks in security protection can be performed best by assigning women.
    B. More women than men are available to fill many vacancies in this position.
    C. The government wants more women in law enforcement because of their better attendance records.
    D. Women can no longer be barred from any government jobs because of sex.

4. The MOST BASIC purpose of patrol by officers is to   4.____

    A. eliminate as much as possible the opportunity for successful misconduct
    B. investigate criminal complaints and accident cases
    C. give prompt assistance to employees and citizens in distress or requesting their help
    D. take persons into custody who commit criminal offenses against persons and property

5. The highest quality of patrol service is MOST generally obtained by   5.____

    A. frequently changing the post assignments of each officer
    B. assigning officers to posts of equal size
    C. assigning problem officers to the least desirable posts
    D. assigning the same officers to the same posts

6. The one of the following requirements which is MOST essential to the successful performance of patrol duty by individual officers is their   6.____

    A. ability to communicate effectively with higher-level officers
    B. prompt signalling according to a prescribed schedule to insure post coverages at all times

1

C. knowledge of post conditions and post hazards
D. willingness to cover large areas during periods of critical manpower shortages

7. Officers on patrol are constantly warned to be on the alert for suspicious persons, actions, and circumstances.
With this in mind, a senior officer should emphasize the need for them to

   A. be cautious and suspicious when dealing officially with any civilian regardless of the latter's overt actions or the circumstances surrounding his dealings with the police
   B. keep looking for the unusual persons, actions, and circumstances on their posts and pay less attention to the usual
   C. take aggressive police action immediately against any unusual person or condition detected on their posts, regardless of any other circumstances
   D. become thoroughly familiar with the usual on their posts so as to be better able to detect the unusual

8. Of primary importance in the safeguarding of property from theft is a good central lock and key issuance and control system.
Which one of the following recommendations about maintaining such a control system would be LEAST acceptable?

   A. In selecting locks to be used for the various gates, building, and storage areas, consideration should be given to the amount of security desired.
   B. Master keys should have no markings that will identify them as such and the list of holders of these keys should be frequently reviewed to determine the continuing necessity for the individuals having them.
   C. Whenever keys for outside doors or gates or for other doors which permit access to important buildings and areas are misplaced, the locks should be immediately changed or replaced pending an investigation.
   D. Whenever an employee fails to return a borrowed key at the time specified, a prompt investigation should be made by the security force.

9. In a crowded building, a fire develops in the basement, and smoke enters the crowded rooms on the first floor. Of the following, the BEST action for an officer to take after an alarm is turned in is to

   A. call out a warning that the building is on fire and that everyone should evacuate because of the immediate danger
   B. call all of the officers together for an emergency meeting and discuss a plan of action
   C. immediately call for assistance from the local police station to help in evacuating the crowd
   D. tell everyone that there is a fire in the building next door and that they should move out onto the streets through available exits

10. Which of the following is in a key position to carry out successfully a safety program of an agency? The

    A. building engineer
    B. bureau chiefs
    C. immediate supervisors
    D. public relations director

11. It is GENERALLY considered that a daily roll call inspection, which checks to see that the officers and their equipment are in good order, is   11._____

    A. *desirable,* chiefly because it informs the superior officer what men will have to purchase new uniforms within a month
    B. *desirable,* chiefly because the public forms their impressions of the organization from the appearance of the officers
    C. *undesirable,* chiefly because this kind of daily inspection unnecessarily delays officers in getting to their assigned patrol posts
    D. *undesirable,* chiefly because roll call inspection usually misses individuals reporting to work late

12. A supervising officer in giving instructions to a group of officers on the principles of accident investigation remarked, "A conclusion that appears reasonable will often be changed by exploring a factor of apparently little importance".   12._____
    Which one of the following precautions does this statement emphasize as MOST important in any accident investigation?

    A. Every accident clue should be fully investigated.
    B. Accidents should not be too promptly investigated.
    C. Only specially trained officers should investigate accidents.
    D. Conclusions about accident causes are highly unreliable.

13. On a rainy day, a senior officer found that 9 of his 50 officers reported to work. What percentage of his officers was ABSENT?   13._____

    A. 18%   B. 80%   C. 82%   D. 90%

14. Officer A and Officer B work at the same post on the same days, but their hours are different. Officer A comes to work at 9:00 A.M. and leaves at 5:00 P.M., with a lunch period between 12:15 P.M. and 1:15 P.M. Officer B comes to work at 10:50 A.M. and works until 6:50 P.M., and he takes an hour for lunch between 3:00 P.M. and 4:00 P.M. What is the total amount of time between 9:00 A.M. and 6:50 P.M. that only ONE officer will be on duty?   14._____

    A. 4 hours   B. 4 hours and 40 minutes
    C. 5 hours   D. 5 hours and 40 minutes

15. An officer's log recorded the following attendance of 30 officers: 15._____

    | Monday | 20 | present; | 10 | absent |
    | Tuesday | 28 | present; | 2 | absent |
    | Wednesday | 30 | present; | 0 | absent |
    | Thursday | 21 | present; | 9 | absent |
    | Friday | 16 | present; | 14 | absent |
    | Saturday | 11 | present; | 19 | absent |
    | Sunday | 14 | present; | 16 | absent |

    On the average, how many men were present on the weekdays (Monday - Friday)?

    A. 21   B. 23   C. 25   D. 27

16. An angry woman is being questioned by an officer when she begins shouting abuses at him.
    The BEST of the following procedures for the officer to follow is to

    A. leave the room until she has cooled off
    B. politely ignore anything she says
    C. place her under arrest by handcuffing her to a fixed object
    D. warn her that he will have to use force to restrain her making remarks

17. Of the following, which is NOT a recommended practice for an officer placing a woman offender under arrest?

    A. Assume that the offender is an innocent and virtuous person and treat her accordingly.
    B. Protect himself from attack by the woman.
    C. Refrain from using excessive physical force on the offender.
    D. Make the public aware that he is not abusing the woman.

Questions 18-21.

DIRECTIONS: Questions 18 through 21 are to be answered SOLELY on the basis of the following passage.

Specific measures for prevention of pilferage will be based on careful analysis of the conditions at each agency. The most practical and effective method to control casual pilferage is the establishment of psychological deterrents.

One of the most common means of discouraging casual pilferage is to search individuals leaving the agency at unannounced times and places. These spot searches may occasionally detect attempts at theft but greater value is realized by bringing to the attention of individuals the fact that they may be apprehended if they do attempt the illegal removal of property.

An aggressive security education program is an effective means of convincing employees that they have much more to lose than they do to gain by engaging in acts of theft. It is important for all employees to realize that pilferage is morally wrong no matter how insignificant the value of the item which is taken. In establishing any deterrent to casual pilferage, security officers must not lose sight of the fact that most employees are honest and disapprove of thievery. Mutual respect between security personnel and other employees of the agency must be maintained if the facility is to be protected from other more dangerous forms of human hazards. Any security measure which infringes on the human rights or dignity of others will jeopardize, rather than enhance, the overall protection of the agency.

18. The $100,000 yearly inventory of an agency revealed that $50 worth of goods had been stolen; the only individuals with access to the stolen materials were the employees. Of the following measures, which would the author of the preceding paragraph MOST likely recommend to a security officer?

    A. Conduct an intensive investigation of all employees to find the culprit.
    B. Make a record of the theft, but take no investigative or disciplinary action against any employee.
    C. Place a tight security check on all future movements of personnel.
    D. Remove the remainder of the material to an area with much greater security.

19. What does the passage imply is the percentage of employees whom a security officer should expect to be honest?   19.____

    A. No employee can be expected to be honest all of the time
    B. Just 50%
    C. Less than 50%
    D. More than 50%

20. According to the passage, the security officer would use which of the following methods to minimize theft in buildings with many exits when his staff is very small?   20.____

    A. Conduct an inventory of all material and place a guard near that which is most likely to be pilfered.
    B. Inform employees of the consequences of legal prosecution for pilfering.
    C. Close off the unimportant exits and have all his men concentrate on a few exits.
    D. Place a guard at each exit and conduct a casual search of individuals leaving the premises.

21. Of the following, the title BEST suited for this passage is: 21.____

    A. Control Measures for Casual Pilfering
    B. Detecting the Potential Pilferer
    C. Financial losses Resulting from Pilfering
    D. The Use of Moral Persuasion in Physical Security

22. Of the following first aid procedures, which will cause the GREATEST harm in treating a fracture?   22.____

    A. Control hemorrhages by applying direct pressure
    B. Keep the broken portion from moving about
    C. Reset a protruding bone by pressing it back into place
    D. Treat the suffering person for shock

23. During a snowstorm, a man comes to you complaining of frostbitten hands.   23.____
    PROPER first aid treatment in this case is to

    A. place the hands under hot running water
    B. place the hands in lukewarm water
    C. call a hospital and wait for medical aid
    D. rub the hands in melting snow

24. While on duty, an officer sees a woman apparently in a state of shock.   24.____
    Of the following, which one is NOT a symptom of shock?

    A. Eyes lacking luster
    B. A cold, moist forehead
    C. A shallow, irregular breathing
    D. A strong, throbbing pulse

25. You notice a man entering your building who begins coughing violently, has shortness of breath, and complains of severe chest pains.   25.____
    These symptoms are GENERALLY indicative of

    A. a heart attack   B. a stroke
    C. internal bleeding   D. an epileptic seizure

26. When an officer is required to record the rolled fingerprint impressions of a prisoner on the standard fingerprint form, the technique recommended by the F.B.I, as MOST likely to result in obtaining clear impressions is to roll

    A. all fingers away from the center of the prisoner's body
    B. all fingers toward the center of the prisoner's body
    C. the thumbs away from and the other fingers toward the center of the prisoner's body
    D. the thumbs toward and the other fingers away from the center of the prisoner's body

26.____

27. The principle which underlies the operation and use of a lie detector machine is that

    A. a person who is not telling the truth will be able to give a consistent story
    B. a guilty mind will unconsciously associate ideas in a very indicative manner
    C. the presence of emotional stress in a person will result in certain abnormal physical reactions
    D. many individuals are not afraid to lie

27.____

Questions 28-32.

DIRECTIONS: Questions 28 through 32 are based SOLELY on the following diagram and the paragraph preceding this group of questions. The paragraph will be divided into two statements. Statement one (1) consists of information given to the senior officer by an agency director; *this information will detail the specific security objectives the senior officer has to meet.* Statement two (2) gives the resources available to the senior officer.

NOTE: The questions are correctly answered only when all of the agency's objectives have been met and when the officer has used all his resources efficiently (i.e., to their maximum effectiveness) in meeting these objectives. All X's in the diagram indicate possible locations of officers' posts. Each X has a corresponding number which is to be used when referring to that location.

DIAGRAM

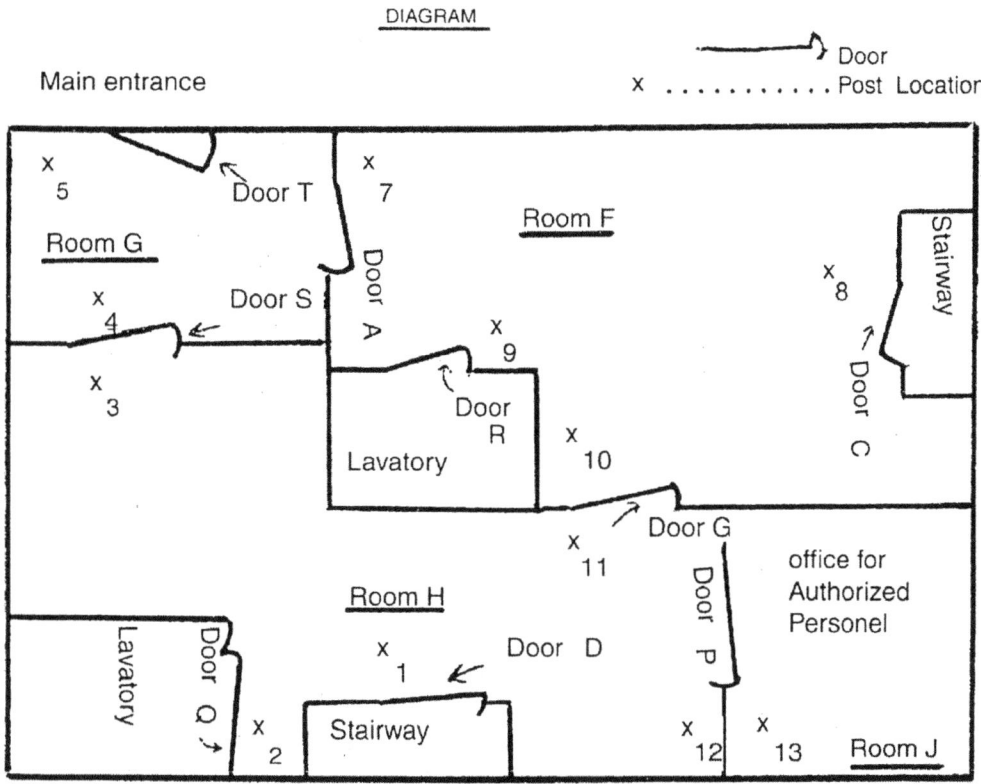

PARAGRAPH

PARAGRAPH

STATEMENT 1: Room G will be the public intake room from which persons will be directed to Room F or Room H; under no circumstances are they to enter the wrong room, and they are not to move from Room F to Room H or vice-versa. A minimum of two officers must be in each room frequented by the public at all times, and they are to keep unauthorized individuals from going to the second floor or into restricted areas. All usable entrances or exits must be covered.

STATEMENT 2: The senior officer can lock any door except the main entrance and stairway doors. He has a staff of five officers to carry out these operations.

NOTE: The senior officer is available for guard duty. Room J is an active office.

28. According to the instructions, how many officers should be assigned inside the office for authorized personnel (Room J)?

    A. 0   B. 1   C. 2   D. 3

28.____

29. In order to keep the public from moving between Room F and Room H, which door(s) can be locked without interfering with normal office operations? Door

    A. G   B. P   C. R and Q   D. S

29.____

30. When placing officers in Room H, the only way the senior officer can satisfy the agency's objectives and his manpower limitations is by placing men at locations

　　A. 1 and 3　　B. 1 and 12　　C. 3 and 11　　D. 11 and 12

31. In accordance with the instructions, the LEAST effective locations to place officers in Room F are locations

　　A. 7 and 9　　B. 7 and 10　　C. 8 and 9　　D. 9 and 10

32. In which room is it MOST difficult for each of the officers to see all the movements of the public? Room

　　A. G　　B. F　　C. H　　D. J

33. According to its own provisions, the Penal Law of the State has a number of general purposes.
It would be LEAST accurate to state that one of these general purposes is to

　　A. give fair warning of the nature of the conduct forbidden and the penalties authorized upon conviction
　　B. define the act or omission and accompanying mental state which constitute each offense
　　C. regulate the procedure which governs the arrest, trial and punishment of convicted offenders
　　D. insure the public safety by preventing the commission of offenses through the deterrent influence of the sentences authorized upon conviction

34. Officers must be well-informed about the meaning of certain terms in connection with their enforcement duties. Which one of the following statements about such terms would be MOST accurate according to the Penal Law of the State? A(n)

　　A. offense is always a crime
　　B. offense is always a violation
　　C. violation is never a crime
　　D. felony is never an offense

35. According to the Penal Law of the State, the one of the following elements which must ALWAYS be present in order to justify the arrest of a person for criminal assault is

　　A. the infliction of an actual physical injury
　　B. an intent to cause an injury
　　C. a threat to inflict a physical injury
　　D. the use of some kind of weapon

36. A recent law of the State defines who are police officers and who are peace officers. The official title of this law is: The

　　A. Criminal Code of Procedure
　　B. Law of Criminal Procedure
　　C. Criminal Procedure Law
　　D. Code of Criminal Procedure

37. If you are required to appear in court to testify as the complainant in a criminal action, it would be MOST important for you to

    A. confine your answers to the questions asked when you are testifying
    B. help the prosecutor even if some exaggeration in your testimony may be necessary
    C. be as fair as possible to the defendant even if some details have to be omitted from your testimony
    D. avoid contradicting other witnesses testifying against the defendant

38. A senior officer is asked by the television news media to explain to the public what happened on his post during an important incident.
    When speaking with departmental permission in front of the tape recorders and cameras, the senior officer can give the MOST favorable impression of himself and his department by

    A. refusing to answer any questions but remaining calm in front of the cameras
    B. giving a detailed report of the wrong decisions made by his agency for handling the particular incident
    C. presenting the appropriate factual information in a competent way
    D. telling what should have been done during the incident and how such incidents will be handled in the future

39. Of the following suggested guidelines for officers, the one which is LEAST likely to be effective in promoting good manners and courtesy in their daily contacts with the public is:

    A. Treat inquiries by telephone in the same manner as those made in person
    B. Never look into the face of the person to whom you are speaking
    C. Never give misinformation in answer to any inquiry on a matter on which you are uncertain of the facts
    D. Show respect and consideration in both trivial and important contacts with the public

40. Assume you are an officer who has had a record of submitting late weekly reports and that you are given an order by your supervisor which is addressed to all line officers. The order states that weekly reports will be replaced by twice-weekly reports.
    The MOST logical conclusion for you to make, of the following, is:

    A. Fully detailed information was missing from your past reports
    B. Most officers have submitted late reports
    C. The supervisor needs more timely information
    D. The supervisor is attempting to punish you for your past late reports

41. A young man with long hair and "mod" clothing makes a complaint to an officer about the rudeness of another officer.
    If the senior officer is not on the premises, the officer receiving the complaint should

    A. consult with the officer who is being accused to see if the youth's story is true
    B. refer the young man to central headquarters
    C. record the complaint made against his fellow officer and ask the youth to wait until he can locate the senior officer
    D. search for the senior officer and bring him back to the site of the complainant

42. During a demonstration, which area should ALWAYS be kept clear of demonstrators? 42.___

    A. Water fountains
    B. Seating areas
    C. Doorways
    D. Restrooms

43. During demonstrations, an officer's MOST important duty is to 43.___

    A. aid the agency's employees to perform their duties
    B. promptly arrest those who might cause incidents
    C. promptly disperse the crowds of demonstrators
    D. keep the demonstrators from disrupting order

44. Of the following, what is the FIRST action a senior officer should take if a demonstration develops in his area without advance warning? 44.___

    A. Call for additional assistance from the police department
    B. Find the leaders of the demonstrators and discuss their demands
    C. See if the demonstrators intend to break the law
    D. Inform his superiors of the event taking place

45. If a senior officer is informed in the morning that a demonstration will take place during the afternoon at his assigned location, he should assemble his officers to discuss the nature and aspects of this demonstration. Of the following, the subject which it is LEAST important to discuss during this meeting is 45.___

    A. making a good impression if an officer is called before the television cameras for a personal interview
    B. the known facts and causes of the demonstration
    C. the attitude and expected behavior of the demonstrators
    D. the individual responsibilities of the officers during the demonstration

46. A male officer has probable reason to believe that a group of women occupying the ladies' toilet are using illicit drugs. 46.___
    The BEST action, of the following, for the officer to take is to

    A. call for assistance and, with the aid of such assistance, enter the toilet and escort the occupants outside
    B. ignore the situation but recommend that the ladies' toilet be closed temporarily
    C. immediately rush into the ladies' toilet and search the occupants therein
    D. knock on the door of the ladies' toilet and ask their permission to enter so that he will not be accused of trying to molest them

47. Assume that you know that a group of demonstrators will not cooperate with your request to throw handbills in a waste basket instead of on the sidewalk. You ask one of the leaders of the group, who agrees with you, to speak to the demonstrators and ask for their cooperation in this matter. 47.___
    Your request of the group leader is

    A. *desirable,* chiefly because an officer needs civilians to control the public since the officer is usually unfriendly to the views of public groups
    B. *undesirable,* chiefly because an officer should never request a civilian to perform his duties
    C. *desirable,* chiefly because the appeal of an acknowledged leader helps in gaining group cooperation

D. *undesirable,* chiefly because an institutional leader is motivated to maneuver a situation to gain his own personal advantage

48. A vague letter received from a female employee in the agency accuses an officer of improper conduct.
The initial investigative interview by the senior officer assigned to check the accusation should GENERALLY be with the

   A. accused officer
   B. female employee
   C. highest superior about disciplinary action against the officer
   D. immediate supervisor of the female employee

48.____

Questions 49-50.

DIRECTIONS: Questions 49 and 50 are to be answered SOLELY on the basis of the information in the following paragraph.

The personal conduct of each member of the Department is the primary factor in promoting desirable police-community relations. Tact, patience, and courtesy shall be strictly observed under all circumstances. A favorable public attitude toward the police must be earned; it is influenced by the personal conduct and attitude of each member of the force, by his personal integrity and courteous manner, by his respect for due process of law, by his devotion to the principles of justice, fairness, and impartiality.

49. According to the preceding paragraph, what is the BEST action an officer can take in dealing with people in a neighborhood?

   A. Assist neighborhood residents by doing favors for them.
   B. Give special attention to the community leaders in order to be able to control them effectively.
   C. Behave in an appropriate manner and give all community members the same just treatment.
   D. Prepare a plan detailing what he, the officer, wants to do for the community and submit it for approval.

49.____

50. As used in the paragraph, the word *impartiality* means *most nearly*

   A. observant   B. unbiased
   C. righteousness   D. honesty

50.____

KEY (CORRECT ANSWERS)

1. B	11. B	21. A	31. D	41. C
2. B	12. A	22. C	32. C	42. C
3. A	13. C	23. B	33. C	43. D
4. A	14. D	24. D	34. C	44. D
5. D	15. B	25. A	35. A	45. A
6. C	16. B	26. D	36. C	46. A
7. D	17. A	27. C	37. A	47. C
8. C	18. B	28. A	38. C	48. B
9. D	19. D	29. A	39. B	49. C
10. C	20. B	30. B	40. C	50. B

TEST 2

DIRECTIONS: Each question or incomplete statement is followed by several suggested answers or completions. Select the one that BEST answers the question or completes the statement. *PRINT THE LETTER OF THE CORRECT ANSWER IN THE SPACE AT THE RIGHT.*

Questions 1-5.

DIRECTIONS: Questions 1 through 5 consist of short paragraphs. Each paragraph contains one word which is INCORRECTLY used because it is NOT in keeping with the meaning of the paragraph. Find the word in each paragraph which is INCORRECTLY used, and then select as the answer the suggested word which should be substituted for the incorrectly used word.

SAMPLE QUESTION

In determining who is to do the work in your unit, you will have to decide just who does what from day to day. One of your lowest responsibilities is to assign work so that everybody gets a fair share and that everyone can do his part well.
    A. new   B. old   C. important   D. performance

EXPLANATION

The word which is NOT in keeping with the meaning of the paragraph is "lowest". This is the INCORRECTLY used word. The suggested word "important" would be in keeping with the meaning of the paragraph and should be substituted for "lowest". Therefore, the CORRECT answer is Choice C.

1. If really good practice in the elimination of preventable injuries is to be achieved and held in any establishment, top management must refuse full and definite responsibility and must apply a good share of its attention to the task.

    A. accept   B. avoidable   C. duties   D. problem

1.____

2. Recording the human face for identification is by no means the only service performed by the camera in the field of investigation. When the trial of any issue takes place, a word picture is sought to be distorted to the court of incidents, occurrences, or events which are in dispute.

    A. appeals   B. description
    C. portrayed   D. deranged

2.____

3. In the collection of physical evidence, it cannot be emphasized too strongly that a haphazard systematic search at the scene of the crime is vital. Nothing must be overlooked. Often the only leads in a case will come from the results of this search.

    A. important   B. investigation
    C. proof   D. thorough

3.____

4. If an investigator has reason to suspect that the witness is mentally stable or a habitual drunkard, he should leave no stone unturned in his investigation to determine if the witness was under the influence of liquor or drugs, or was mentally unbalanced either at the time of the occurrence to which he testified or at the time of the trial.

    A. accused   B. clue   C. deranged   D. question

4.____

13

5. The use of records is a valuable step in crime investigation and is the main reason every department should maintain accurate reports. Crimes are not committed through the use of departmental records alone but from the use of all records, of almost every type, wherever they may be found and whenever they give any incidental information regarding the criminal.

   A. accidental   B. necessary   C. reported   D. solved

Questions 6-8.

DIRECTIONS: Questions 6 through 8 are to be answered SOLELY on the basis of the following passage.

The mass media are an integral part of the daily life of virtually every American. Among these media, the youngest, television, is the most persuasive. Ninety-five percent of American homes have at least one television set, and on the average that set is in use for about 40 hours each week. The central place of television in American life makes this medium the focal point of a growing national concern over the effects of media portrayals of violence on the values, attitudes, and behavior of an ever increasing audience.

In our concern about violence and its causes, it is easy to make television a scapegoat. But we emphasise the fact that there is no simple answer to the problem of violence -- no single explanation of its causes, and no single prescription for its control. It should be remembered that America also experienced high levels of crime and violence in periods before the advent of television.

The problem of balance, taste, and artistic merit in entertaining programs on television are complex. We cannot <u>countenance</u> government censorship of television. Nor would we seek to impose arbitrary limitations on programming which might jeopardize television's ability to deal in dramatic presentations with controversial social issues. Nonetheless, we are deeply troubled by television's constant portrayal of violence, not in any genuine attempt to focus artistic expression on the human condition, but rather in pandering to a public preoccupation with violence that television itself has helped to generate.

6. According to the passage, television uses violence MAINLY

   A. to highlight the reality of everyday existence
   B. to satisfy the audience's hunger for destructive action
   C. to shape the values and attitudes of the public
   D. when it films documentaries concerning human conflict

7. Which one of the following statements is BEST supported by this passage?

   A. Early American history reveals a crime pattern which is not related to television.
   B. Programs should give presentations of social issues and never portray violent acts.
   C. Television has proven that entertainment programs can easily make the balance between taste and artistic merit a simple matter.
   D. Values and behavior should be regulated by governmental censorship.

8. Of the following, which word has the same meaning as <u>countenance</u> as it is used in the above passage?

   A. approve   B. exhibit   C. oppose   D. reject

Questions 9-12.

DIRECTIONS: Questions 9 through 12 are to be answered SOLELY on the basis of the following graph relating to the burglary rate in the city, 2003 to 2008, inclusive.

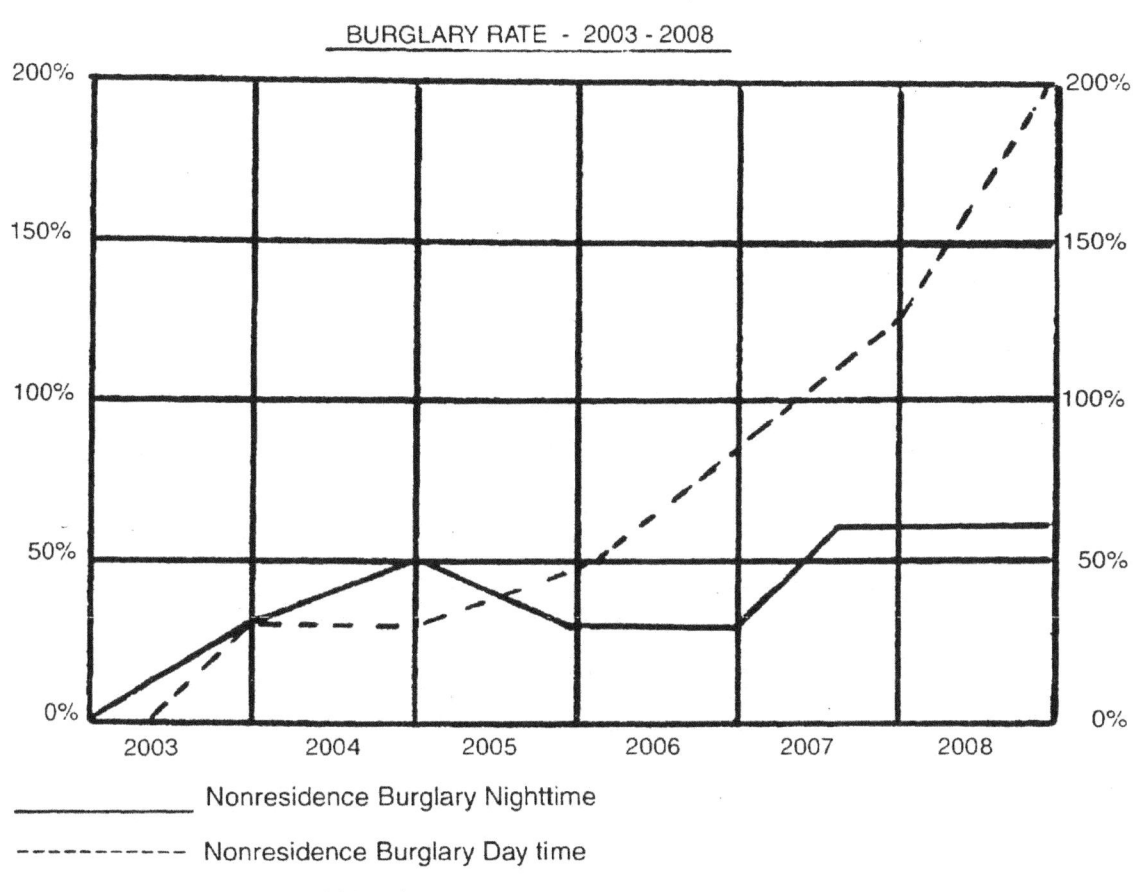

9. At the beginning of what year was the percentage increase in daytime and nighttime burglaries the SAME?

   A. 2004   B. 2005   C. 2006   D. 2008

10. In what year did the percentage of nighttime burglaries DECREASE?

    A. 2003   B. 2005   C. 2006   D. 2008

11. In what year was there the MOST rapid increase in the percentage of daytime non-residence burglaries?

    A. 2004   B. 2006   C. 2007   D. 2008

12. At the end of 2007, the actual number of nighttime burglaries committed

    A. was about 20%
    B. was 40%
    C. was 400
    D. cannot be determined from the information given

Questions 13-17.

DIRECTIONS: Questions 13 through 17 consist of two sentences numbered 1 and 2 taken from police officers' reports. Some of these sentences are correct according to ordinary formal English usage. Other sentences are incorrect because they contain errors in English usage or punctuation. Consider a sentence correct if it contains no errors in English usage or punctuation even if there may be other ways of writing the sentence correctly. Mark your answer to each question in the space at the right as follows:

    A. If only sentence 1 is correct, but not sentence 2
    B. If only sentence 2 is correct, but not sentence 1
    C. If sentences 1 and 2 are both correct
    D. If sentences 1 and 2 are both incorrect

SAMPLE QUESTION
1. The woman claimed that the purse was her's.
2. Everyone of the new officers was assigned to a patrol post.

EXPLANATION

Sentence 1 is INCORRECT because of an error in punctuation. The possessive words, "ours, yours, hers, theirs," do not have the apostrophe (').

Sentence 2 is CORRECT because the subject of the sentence is "Everyone" which is singular and requires the singular verb "was assigned".

Since only sentence 2 is correct, but not sentence 1, the CORRECT answer is B.

13. 1. Either the patrolman or his sergeant are always ready to help the public.
     2. The sergeant asked the patrolman when he would finish the report.

14. 1. The injured man could not hardly talk.
     2. Every officer had ought to hand in their reports on time.

15. 1. Approaching the victim of the assault, two large bruises were noticed by me.
     2. The prisoner was arrested for assault, resisting arrest, and use of a deadly weapon.

16. 1. A copy of the orders, which had been prepared by the captain, was given to each patrolman.
     2. It's always necessary to inform an arrested person of his constitutional rights before asking him any questions.

17. 1. To prevent further bleeding, I applied a tourniquet tothe wound.
     2. John Rano a senior officer was on duty at the time of the accident.

Questions 18-25.

DIRECTIONS: Answer each of Questions 18 through 25 SOLELY on the basis of the statement preceding the questions.

18. The criminal is one whose habits have been erroneously developed or, we should say, developed in anti-social patterns, and therefore the task of dealing with him is not one of punishment, but of treatment.
The basic principle expressed in this statement is BEST illustrated by the

    A. emphasis upon rehabilitation in penal institutions
    B. prevalence of capital punishment for murder
    C. practice of imposing heavy fines for minor violations
    D. legal provision for trial by jury in criminal cases

19. The writ of habeas corpus is one of the great guarantees of personal liberty. Of the following, the BEST justification for this statement is that the writ of habeas corpus is frequently used to   19.____

    A. compel the appearance in court of witnesses who are outside the state
    B. obtain the production of books and records at a criminal trial
    C. secure the release of a person improperly held in custody
    D. prevent the use of deception in obtaining testimony of reluctant witnesses

20. Fifteen persons suffered effects of carbon dioxide asphyxiation shortly before noon recently in a seventh-floor pressing shop. The accident occurred in a closed room where six steam presses were in operation. Four men and one woman were overcome.   20.____
    Of the following, the MOST probable reason for the fact that so many people were affected simultaneously is that

    A. women evidently show more resistance to the effects of carbon dioxide than men
    B. carbon dioxide is an odorless and colorless gas
    C. carbon dioxide is lighter than air
    D. carbon dioxide works more quickly at higher altitudes

21. Lay the patient on his stomach, one arm extended directly overhead, the other arm bent at the elbow, and with the face turned outward and resting on hand or forearm.   21.____
    To the officer who is skilled at administering first aid, these instructions should IMMEDIATELY suggest

    A. application of artificial respiration
    B. treatment for third degree burns of the arm
    C. setting a dislocated shoulder
    D. control of capillary bleeding in the stomach

22. The soda and acid fire extinguisher is the hand extinguisher most commonly used by officers. The main body of the cylinder is filled with a mixture of water and bicarbonate of soda. In a separate interior compartment, at the top, is a small bottle of sulphuric acid. When the extinguisher is inverted, the acid spills into the solution below and starts a chemical reaction. The carbon dioxide thereby generated forces the solution from the extinguisher.   22.____
    The officer who understands the operation of this fire extinguisher should know that it is LEAST likely to operate properly

    A. in basements or cellars
    B. in extremely cold weather
    C. when the reaction is of a chemical nature
    D. when the bicarbonate of soda is in solution

23. Suppose that, at a training lecture, you are told that many of the men in our penal institutions today are second and third offenders.   23.____
    Of the following, the MOST valid inference you can make SOLELY on the basis of this statement is that

    A. second offenders are not easily apprehended
    B. patterns of human behavior are not easily changed
    C. modern laws are not sufficiently flexible
    D. laws do not breed crimes

24. In all societies of our level of culture, acts are committed which arouse censure severe enough to take the form of punishment by the government. Such acts are crimes, not because of their inherent nature, but because of their ability to arouse resentment and to stimulate repressive measures.
Of the following, the MOST valid inference which can be drawn from this statement is that

    A. society unjustly punishes acts which are inherently criminal
    B. many acts are not crimes but are punished by society because such acts threaten the lives of innocent people
    C. only modern society has a level of culture
    D. societies sometimes disagree as to what acts are crimes

25. Crime cannot be measured directly. Its amount must be inferred from the frequency of some occurrence connected with it; for example, crimes brought to the attention of the police, persons arrested, prosecutions, convictions, and other dispositions, such as probation or commitment. Each of these may be used as an index of the amount of crime.
SOLELY on the basis of the foregoing statement, it is MOST correct to state that

    A. the incidence of crime cannot be estimated with any accuracy
    B. the number of commitments is usually greater than the number of probationary sentences
    C. the amount of crime is ordinarily directly correlated with the number of persons arrested
    D. a joint consideration of crimes brought to the attention of the police and the number of prosecutions undertaken gives little indication of the amount of crime in a locality

KEY (CORRECT ANSWERS)

1.	B	11.	D
2.	A	12.	D
3.	D	13.	D
4.	C	14.	D
5.	D	15.	B
6.	B	16.	C
7.	A	17.	A
8.	A	18.	A
9.	A	19.	C
10.	B	20.	B

21. A
22. B
23. B
24. D
25. C

EXAMINATION SECTION
TEST 1

DIRECTIONS: Each question or incomplete statement is followed by several suggested answers or completions. Select the one that BEST answers the question or completes the statement. *PRINT THE LETTER OF THE CORRECT ANSWER IN THE SPACE AT THE RIGHT.*

Questions 1-4.

DIRECTIONS: Questions 1 through 4 are based on the picture entitled *Contents of a Woman's Handbag*. Assume that all of the contents are shown in the picture.

CONTENTS OF A WOMAN'S HANDBAG

1. Where does Gladys Constantine live?

    A. Chalmers Street in Manhattan
    B. Summer Street in Manhattan
    C. Summer Street in Brooklyn
    D. Chalmers Street in Brooklyn

2. How many keys were in the handbag?

    A. 2   B. 3   C. 4   D. 5

3. How much money was in the handbag? _____ dollar(s).

    A. Exactly five   B. More than five
    C. Exactly ten   D. Less than one

4. The sales slip found in the handbag shows the purchase of which of the following?

    A. The handbag   B. Lipstick
    C. Tissues   D. Prescription medicine

Questions 5-8.

DIRECTIONS: Questions 5 through 8 are based on the floor plan below.

FLOOR PLAN

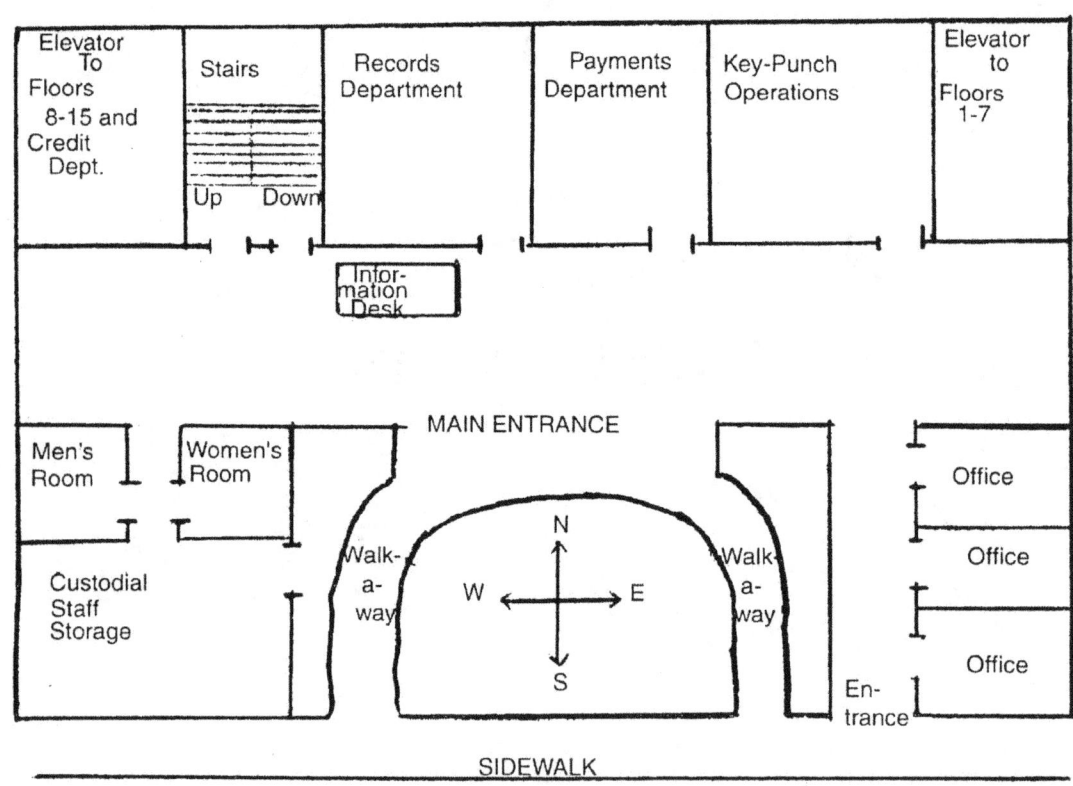

5. A special officer (security officer) on duty at the main entrance must be aware of other outside entrances to his area of the building. These unguarded entrances are usually kept locked, but they are important in case of fire or other emergency.
Besides the main entrance, how many OTHER entrances shown on the floor plan directly face Forty-ninth Street?
_____ other entrances.

   A. No   B. One   C. Two   D. Three

6. A person who arrives at the main entrance and asks to be directed to the Credit Department SHOULD be told to

   A. take the elevator on the left
   B. take the elevator on the right
   C. go to a different entrance
   D. go up the stairs on the left

7. On the east side of the entrance can be found

   A. a storage room   B. offices
   C. toilets   D. stairs

8. The space DIRECTLY BEHIND the Information Desk in the floor plan is occupied by

   A. up and down stairs   B. key punch operations
   C. toilets   D. the records department

Questions 9-12.

DIRECTIONS: Answer Questions 9 to 12 on the basis of the information given in the passage below.

The public often believes that the main job of a uniformed officer is to enforce laws by simply arresting people. In reality, however, many of the situations that an officer deals with do not call for the use of his arrest power. In the first place, an officer spends much of his time <u>preventing</u> crimes from happening, by spotting potential violations or suspicious behavior and taking action to prevent illegal acts. In the second place, many of the situations in which officers are called on for assistance involve elements like personal arguments, husband-wife quarrels, noisy juveniles, or mentally disturbed persons. The majority of these problems do not result in arrests and convictions, and often they do not even involve illegal behavior. In the third place, even in situations where there seems to be good reason to make an arrest, an officer may have to exercise very good judgment. There are times when making an arrest too soon could touch off a riot, or could result in the detention of a minor offender while major offenders escaped, or could cut short the gathering of necessary on-the-scene evidence.

9. The above passage IMPLIES that most citizens

   A. will start to riot if they see an arrest being made
   B. appreciate the work that law enforcement officers do
   C. do not realize that making arrests is only a small part of law enforcement
   D. never call for assistance unless they are involved in a personal argument or a husband-wife quarrel

10. According to the passage, one way in which law enforcement officers can prevent crimes from happening is by

    A. arresting suspicious characters
    B. letting minor offenders go free
    C. taking action on potential violations
    D. refusing to get involved in husband-wife fights

11. According to the passage, which of the following statements is NOT true of situations involving mentally disturbed persons?

    A. It is a waste of time to call on law enforcement officers for assistance in such situations.
    B. Such situations may not involve illegal behavior
    C. Such situations often do not result in arrests.
    D. Citizens often turn to law enforcement officers for help in such situations.

12. The last sentence in the passage mentions *detention of minor offenders.*
    Of the following, which BEST explains the meaning of the word *detention* as used here?

    A. Sentencing someone
    B. Indicting someone
    C. Calling someone before a grand jury
    D. Arresting someone

Questions 13-28.

DIRECTIONS: In answering Questions 13 through 28, assume that *you* means a special officer (security officer) on duty. Your basic responsibilities are safeguarding people and property and maintaining order in the area to which you are assigned. You are in uniform, and you are not armed. You keep in touch with your supervisory station either by telephone or by a two-way radio (walkie-talkie).

13. It is a general rule that if the security alarm goes off showing that someone has made an unlawful entrance into a building, no officer responsible for security shall proceed to investigate alone. Each officer must be accompanied by at least one other officer.
    Of the following, which is the MOST probable reason for this rule?

    A. It is dangerous for an officer to investigate such a situation alone.
    B. The intruder might try to bribe an officer to let him go.
    C. One officer may be inexperienced and needs an experienced partner.
    D. Two officers are better than one officer in writing a report of the investigation.

14. You are on weekend duty on the main floor of a public building. The building is closed to the public on weekends, but some employees are sometimes asked to work weekends. You have been instructed to use cautious good judgment in opening the door for such persons.
    Of the following, which one MOST clearly shows the poorest judgment?

A. Admitting an employee who is personally known to you without asking to see any identification except the permit slip signed by the employee's supervisor
B. Refusing to admit someone whom you do not recognize but who claims left his identification at home
C. Admitting to the building only those who can give a detailed description of their weekend work duties
D. Leaving the entrance door locked for a while to make regulation security checks of other areas in the building with the result that no one can either enter or leave during these periods

15. You are on duty at a public building. An office employee tells you that she left her purse in her desk when she went out to lunch, and she has just discovered that it is gone. She has been back from lunch for half an hour and has not left her desk during this period. What should you do FIRST?

    A. Warn all security personnel to stop any suspicious-looking person who is seen with a purse
    B. Ask for a description of the purse
    C. Call the Lost and Found and ask if a purse has been turned in
    D. Obtain statements from any employees who were in the office during the lunch hour

16. You are patrolling your assigned area in a public building. You hear a sudden crash and the sound of running footsteps. You investigate and find that someone has forced open a locked entrance to the building. What is the FIRST thing you should do?

    A. Close the door and try to fix the lock so that no one else can get in
    B. Use your two-way radio to report the emergency and summon help
    C. Chase after the person whose running footsteps you heard
    D. Go immediately to your base office and make out a brief written report

17. You and another special officer (security officer) are on duty in the main waiting area at a welfare center. A caseworker calls both of you over and whispers that one of the clients, Richard Roe, may be carrying a gun. Of the following, what is the BEST action for both of you to take?

    A. You should approach the man, one on each side, and one of you should say loudly and clearly, *"Richard Roe, you are under arrest."*
    B. Both of you should ask the man to go with you to a private room, and then find out if he is carrying a gun
    C. Both of you should grab him, handcuff him, and take him to the nearest precinct station house
    D. Both of you should watch him carefully but not do anything unless he actually pulls a gun

18. You are on duty at a welfare center. You are told that a caseworker is being threatened by a man with a knife. You go immediately to the scene, and you find the caseworker lying on the floor with blood spurting from a wound in his arm. You do not know who the attacker is. What should you do FIRST?

    A. Ask the caseworker for a description of the attacker so that you can set out in pursuit and try to catch him
    B. Take down the names and addresses of any witnesses to the incident

C. Give first aid to the caseworker, if you can, and immediately call for an ambulance
D. Search the people standing around in the room for the knife

19. As a special officer (security officer), you have been patrolling a special section of a hospital building for a week. Smoking is not allowed in this section because the oxygen tanks in use here could easily explode. However, you have observed that some employees sneak into the linen-supply room in this section in order to smoke without anybody seeing them.
Of the following, which is the BEST way for you to deal with this situation?

   A. Whenever you catch anyone smoking, call his supervisor immediately
   B. Request the Building Superintendent to put a padlock on the door of the linen-supply room
   C. Ignore the smoking because you do not want to get a reputation for interfering in the private affairs of other employees
   D. Report the situation to your supervisor and follow his instructions

19.____

20. You are on duty at a hospital. You have been assigned to guard the main door, and you are responsible for remaining at your post until relieved. On one of the wards for which you are not responsible, there is a patient who was wounded in a street fight. This patient is under arrest for killing another man in this fight, and he is supposed to be under round-the-clock police guard. A nurse tells you that one of the police officers assigned to guard the patient has suddenly taken ill and has to periodically leave his post to go to the washroom. The nurse is worried because she thinks the patient might try to escape.
Of the following, which is the BEST action for you to take?

   A. Tell the nurse to call you whenever the police officer leaves his post so that you can keep an eye on the patient while the officer is gone
   B. Assume that the police officer probably knows his job, and that there is no reason for you to worry
   C. Alert your supervisor to the nurse's report
   D. Warn the police officer that the nurse has been talking about him

20.____

21. You are on night duty at a hospital where you are responsible for patrolling a large section of the main building. Your supervisor tells you that there have been several nighttime thefts from a supply room in your section and asks you to be especially alert for suspicious activity near this supply room.
Of the following, which is the MOST reasonable way to carry out your supervisor's direction?

   A. Check the supply room regularly at half-hour intervals
   B. Make frequent checks of the supply room at irregular intervals
   C. Station yourself by the door of the supply room and stay at this post all night
   D. Find a hidden spot from which you can watch the supply room and stay there all night

21.____

22. You are on duty at a vehicle entrance to a hospital. Parking space on the hospital grounds is strictly limited, and no one is ever allowed to park there unless they have an official parking permit. You have just stopped a driver who does not have a parking permit, but he explains that
he is a doctor and he has a patient in the hospital. What should you do?

22.____

A. Let him park since he has explained that he is a doctor
B. Ask in a friendly way, *"Can I check your identification?"*
C. Call the Information Desk to make sure there is such a patient in the hospital
D. Tell the driver politely but firmly that he will have to park somewhere else

23. You are on duty at a public building. A man was just mugged on a stairway. The mugger took the man's wallet and started to run down the stairs but tripped and fell. Now the mugger is lying unconscious at the bottom of the stairs and bleeding from the mouth.
The FIRST thing you should do is to

    A. search him to see if he is carrying any other stolen property
    B. pick him up and carry him away from the stairs
    C. try and revive him for questioning
    D. put in a call for an ambulance and police assistance

24. After someone breaks into an employee's locker at a public building, you interview the employee to determine what is missing from the locker. The employee becomes hysterical and asks why you are *wasting time with all these questions* instead of going after the thief.
The MOST reasonable thing for you to do is

    A. tell the employee that it is very important to have an accurate description of the missing articles
    B. quietly tell the employee to calm down and stop interfering with your work
    C. explain to the employee that you are only doing what you were told to do and that you don't make the rules
    D. assure the employee that there are a lot of people working on the case and that someone else is probably arresting the thief right now

25. You are on duty at a public building. An employee reports that a man has just held her up and taken her money. The employee says that the man was about 25 years old, with short blond hair and a pale complexion and was wearing blue jeans.
Of the following additional facts, which one would probably be MOST valuable to officers searching the building for the suspect?

    A. The man was wearing dark glasses.
    B. He had on a green jacket.
    C. He was about 5 feet 8 inches tall.
    D. His hands and fingernails were very dirty.

26. When the fire alarm goes off, it is your job as a special officer (security officer) to see that all employees leave the building quickly by the correct exits. A fire alarm has just sounded, and you are checking the offices on one of the floors. A supervisor in one office tells you, *"This is probably just another fire drill. I've sent my office staff out, but I don't want to stop my own work."*
What should you do?

    A. Insist politely but firmly that the supervisor must obey the fire rules.
    B. Tell the supervisor that it is all right this time but that the rules must be followed in the future.
    C. Tell the supervisor that he is under arrest.
    D. Allow the supervisor to do as he sees fit since he is in charge of his own office.

27. You are on duty on the main floor of a public building. You have been informed that a briefcase has just been stolen from an office on the tenth floor. You see a man getting off the elevator with a briefcase that matches the description of the one that was stolen. What is the FIRST action you should take?

    A. Arrest the man and take him to the nearest public station
    B. Stop the man and say politely that you want to take a look at the briefcase
    C. Take the briefcase from the man and tell him that he cannot have it back unless he can prove that it is his
    D. Do not stop the man but note down his description and the exact time he got off the elevator

28. You are on duty at a welfare center. You have been told that two clients are arguing with a caseworker and making loud threats. You go to the scene, but the caseworker tells you that everything is now under control. The two clients, who are both mean-looking characters, are still there but seem to be acting normally.
    What SHOULD you do?

    A. Apologize for having made a mistake and go away.
    B. Arrest the two men for having caused a disturbance.
    C. Insist on standing by until the interview is over, then escort the two men from the building.
    D. Leave the immediate scene but watch for any further developments.

29. You are on duty at a welfare center. A client comes up to you and says that two men just threatened him with a knife and made him give them his money. The client has alcohol on his breath and he is shabbily dressed. He points out the two men he says took the money.
    Of the following, which is the BEST action to take?

    A. Arrest the two men on the client's complaint.
    B. Ignore the client's complaint since he doesn't look as if he could have had any money.
    C. Suggest to the client that he may be imagining things.
    D. Investigate and find out what happened.

Questions 30-35.

DIRECTIONS: Answer Questions 30 through 35 on the basis of the information given in the passage below. Assume that all questions refer to the same state described in the passage.

The courts and the police consider an "offense" as any conduct that is punishable by a fine or imprisonment. Such offenses include many kinds of acts - from behavior that is merely annoying, like throwing a noisy party that keeps everyone awake, all the way up to violent acts like murder. The law classifies offenses according to the penalties that are provided for them. In one state, minor offenses are called "violations." A violation is punishable by a fine of not more than $250 or imprisonment of not more than 15 days, or both. The annoying behavior mentioned above is an example of a violation. More serious offenses are classified as "crimes." Crimes are classified by the kind of penalty that is provided. A "misdemeanor" is a crime that is punishable by a fine of not more than $1,000 or by imprisonment of not more than one year, or both. Examples of misdemeanors include stealing something with a value of $100 or less, turning in a false alarm, or illegally possessing less than 1/8 of an ounce of a dangerous drug. A "felony" is a criminal offense punishable by imprisonment of more than one year. Murder is clearly a felony.

30. According to the above passage, any act that is punishable by imprisonment or by a fine is called a(n)

    A. offense   B. violation   C. crime   D. felony

31. According to the above passage, which of the following is classified as a crime?

    A. Offense punishable by 15 days imprisonment
    B. Minor offense
    C. Violation
    D. Misdemeanor

32. According to the above passage, if a person guilty of burglary can receive a prison sentence of 7 years or more, burglary would be classified as a

    A. violation   B. misdemeanor
    C. felony   D. violent act

33. According to the above passage, two offenses that would BOTH be classified as misdemeanors are

    A. making unreasonable noise and stealing a $90 bicycle
    B. stealing a $75 radio and possessing 1/16 of an ounce of heroin
    C. holding up a bank and possessing 1/4 of a pound of marijuana
    D. falsely reporting a fire and illegally double-parking

34. The above passage says that offenses are classified according to the penalties provided for them.
    On the basis of clues in the passage, who probably decides what the maximum penalties should be for the different kinds of offenses?

    A. The State lawmakers   B. The City police
    C. The Mayor   D. Officials in Washington, B.C.

35. Of the following, which BEST describes the subject matter of the passage?

    A. How society deals with criminals
    B. How offenses are classified
    C. Three types of criminal behavior
    D. The police approach to offenders

KEY (CORRECT ANSWERS)

1. C
2. C
3. B
4. D
5. B

6. A
7. B
8. D
9. C
10. C

11. A
12. D
13. A
14. C
15. B

16. B
17. B
18. C
19. D
20. C

21. B
22. D
23. D
24. A
25. C

26. A
27. B
28. D
29. D
30. A

31. D
32. C
33. B
34. A
35. B

TEST 2

DIRECTIONS: Each question or incomplete statement is followed by several suggested answers or completions. Select the one that BEST answers the question or completes the statement. *PRINT THE LETTER OF THE CORRECT ANSWER IN THE SPACE AT THE RIGHT.*

Questions 1-5.

DIRECTIONS: Questions 1 through 5 are based on the drawing below showing a view of a waiting area in a public building.

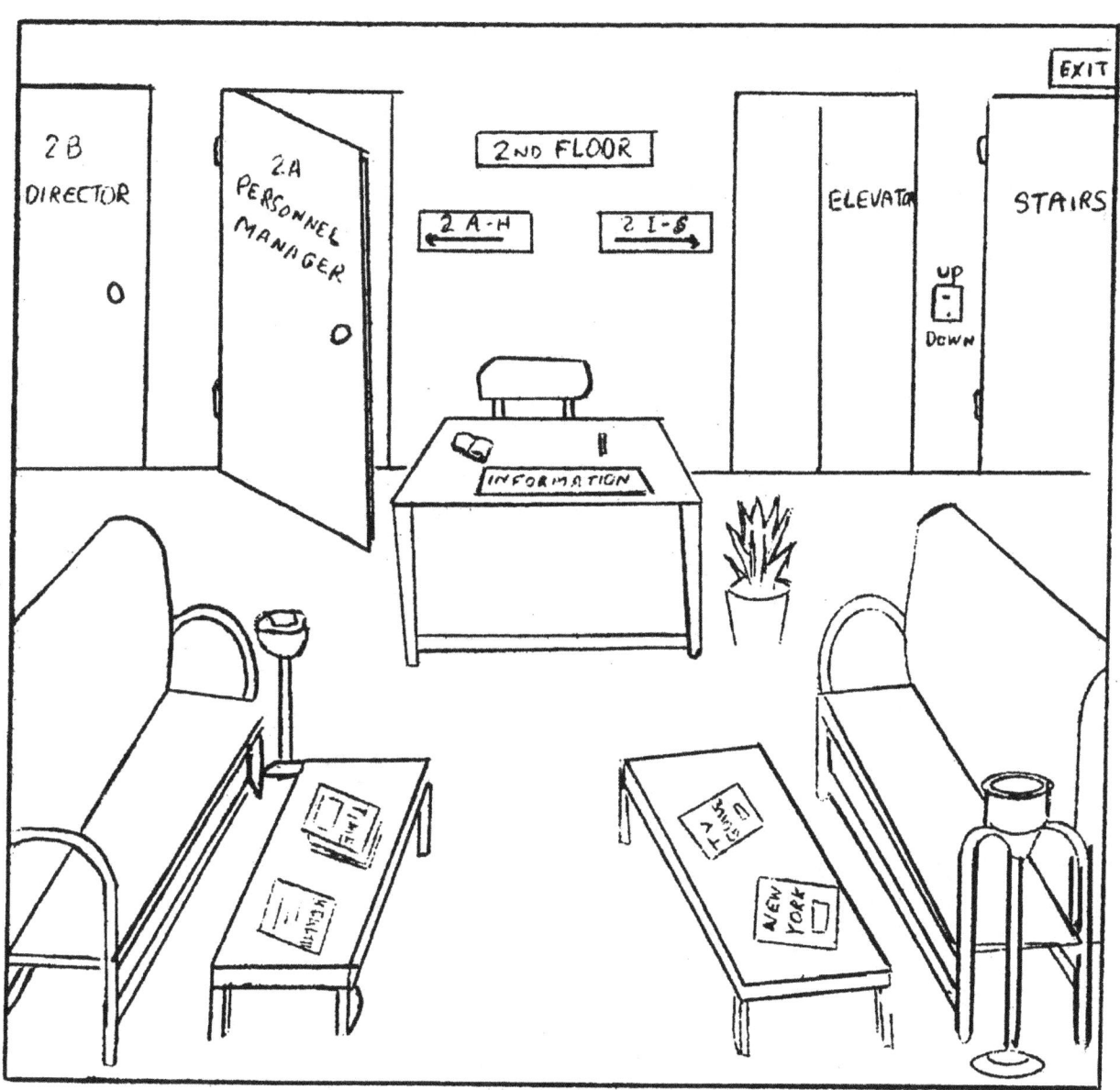

1. A desk is shown in the drawing. Which of the following is on the desk? A(n) 1._____

    A. plant   B. telephone
    C. In-Out file   D. *Information* sign

31

2. On which floor is the waiting area?

   A. Basement
   B. Main floor
   C. Second floor
   D. Third floor

3. The door IMMEDIATELY TO THE RIGHT of the desk is a(n)

   A. door to the Personnel Office
   B. elevator door
   C. door to another corridor
   D. door to the stairs

4. Among the magazines on the tables in the waiting area are

   A. TIME and NEWSWEEK
   B. READER'S DIGEST and T.V. GUIDE
   C. NEW YORK and READER'S DIGEST
   D. TIME and T.V. GUIDE

5. One door is partly open. This is the door to

   A. the Director's office
   B. the Personnel Manager's office
   C. the stairs
   D. an unmarked office

Questions 6-9.

DIRECTIONS: Questions 6 through 9 are based on the drawing below showing the contents of a male suspect's pockets.

CONTENTS OF A MALE SUSPECT'S POCKETS

6. The suspect had a slip in his pockets showing an appointment at an out-patient clinic on   6._____

   A. February 9, 2013
   B. September 2, 2013
   C. February 19, 2013
   D. September 12, 2013

7. The MP3 player that was found on the suspect was made by   7._____

   A. RCA   B. GE   C. Sony   D. Zenith

8. The coins found in the suspect's pockets have a TOTAL value of   8._____

   A. 56¢   B. 77¢   C. $1.05   D. $1.26

9. All except one of the following were found in the suspect's pockets.   9._____
   Which was NOT found? A

   A. ticket stub
   B. comb
   C. subway fare
   D. pen

Questions 10-18

DIRECTIONS: In answering Questions 10 through 18, assume that *you* means a special officer (security officer) on duty. Your basic responsibilities are safeguarding people and property and maintaining order in the area to which you are assigned. You are in uniform, and you are not armed. You keep in touch with your supervisory station either by telephone or by a two-way radio (a walkie-talkie).

10. You are on duty at a center run by the Department of Social Services. Two teenaged   10._____
    boys are on their way out of the center. As they go past you, they look at you and laugh, and one makes a remark to you in Spanish. You do not understand Spanish, but you suspect it was a nasty remark.
    What SHOULD you do?

    A. Give the boys a lecture about showing respect for a uniform.
    B. Tell the boys that they had better stay away from the center from now on.
    C. Call for an interpreter and insist that the boy repeat the remark to the interpreter.
    D. Let the boys go on their way since they have done nothing requiring your intervention.

11. You are on duty at a shelter run by the Department of Social Services. You know that   11._____
    many of the shelter clients have drinking problems, drug problems, or mental health problems. You get a call for assistance from a caseworker who says a fight has broken out. When you arrive on the scene, you see that about a dozen clients are engaged in a free-for-all and that two or three of them have pulled knives.
    The BEST course of action is to

    A. call for additional assistance and order all bystanders away from the area
    B. jump into the center of the fighting group and try to separate the fighters
    C. pick up a heavy object and start swinging at anybody who has a knife
    D. try to find out what clients started the fight and place them under arrest

4 (#2)

12. You have been assigned to duty at a children's shelter run by the Department of Social Services. The children range in age from 6 to 15, and many of them are at the shelter because they have no homes to go to.
Of the following, which is the BEST attitude for you to take in dealing with these youngsters?

   A. Assume that they admire and respect anyone in uniform and that they will not usually give you much trouble
   B. Assume that they fear and distrust anyone in uniform and that they are going to give you a hard time unless you act tough
   C. Expect that many of them are going to become juvenile delinquents because of their bad backgrounds and that you should be suspicious of everything they do
   D. Expect that many of them may be emotionally upset and that you should be alert for unusual behavior

13. You are on duty outside the emergency room of a hospital. You notice that an old man has been sitting on a bench outside the room for a long time. He arrived alone, and he has not spoken to anyone at all.
What SHOULD you do?

   A. Pay no attention to him since he is not bothering anyone.
   B. Tell him to leave since he does not seem to have any business there.
   C. Ask him if you can help him in any way.
   D. Do not speak to him, but keep an eye on him.

14. You are patrolling a section of a public building. An elderly woman carrying a heavy shopping bag asks you if you would watch the shopping bag for her while she keeps an appointment in the building.
What SHOULD you do?

   A. Watch the shopping bag for her since her appointment probably will not take long.
   B. Refuse her request, explaining that your duties keep you on the move.
   C. Agree to her request just to be polite, but then continue your patrol after the woman is out of sight.
   D. Find a bystander who will agree to watch the shopping bag for her.

15. You are on duty at a public building. It is nearly 6:00 P.M., and most employees have left for the day.
You see two well-dressed men carrying an office calculating machine out of the building. You SHOULD

   A. stop them and ask for an explanation
   B. follow them to see where they are going
   C. order them to put down the machine and leave the building immediately
   D. take no action since they do not look like burglars

16. You are on duty patrolling a public building. You have just tripped on the stairs and turned your ankle. The ankle hurts and is starting to swell.
What is the BEST thing to do?

A. Take a taxi to a hospital emergency room, and from there have a hospital employee call your supervisor to explain the situation.
B. First try soaking your foot in cold water for half an hour, then go off duty if you really cannot walk at all.
C. Report the situation to your supervisor, explaining that you need prompt medical attention for your ankle.
D. Find a place where you can sit until you are due to go off duty, then have a doctor look at your ankle.

17. One of your duties as a special officer (security officer) on night patrol in a public building is to check the washrooms to see that the taps are turned off and that there are no plumbing leaks.
Of the following possible reasons for this inspection, which is probably the MOST important reason?

    A. If the floor gets wet, someone might slip and fall the next morning.
    B. A running water tap might be a sign that there is an intruder in the building.
    C. A washroom flood could leak through the ceilings and walls below and cause a lot of damage.
    D. Leaks must be reported quickly so that repairs can be scheduled as soon as possible.

18. You are on duty at a public building. A department supervisor tells you that someone has left a suspicious-looking package in the hallway on his floor. You investigate, and you hear ticking in the parcel. You think it could be a bomb.
The FIRST thing you should do is to

    A. rapidly question employees on this floor to get a description of the person who left the package
    B. write down the description of the package and the name of the department supervisor
    C. notify your security headquarters that there may be a bomb in the building and that all personnel should be evacuated
    D. pick up the package carefully and remove it from the building as quickly as you can

Questions 19-22.

DIRECTIONS: Answer Questions 19 through 22 on the basis of the Fact Situation and the Report of Arrest form below. Questions 19 through 22 ask how the report form should be filled in based on the information given in the Fact Situation.

FACT SITUATION

Jesse Stein is a special officer (security officer) who is assigned to a welfare center at 435 East Smythe Street, Brooklyn. He was on duty there Thursday morning, February 1. At 10:30 A.M., a client named Jo Ann Jones, 40 years old, arrived with her ten-year-old son, Peter. Another client, Mary Alice Wiell, 45 years old, immediately began to insult Mrs. Jones. When Mrs. Jones told her to "go away," Mrs. Wiell pulled out a long knife. The special officer (security officer) intervened and requested Mrs. Wiell to drop the knife. She would not, and he had to use necessary force to disarm her. He arrested her on charges of disorderly conduct, harassment, and possession of a dangerous weapon. Mrs. Wiell lives at 118 Heally Street,

Brooklyn, Apartment 4F, and she is unemployed. The reason for her aggressive behavior is not known.

REPORT OF ARREST	
01) _____ (Prisoner's surname) (first) (initial)	(08) _____ (Precinct)
(02) _____ (Address)	(09) _____ (Date of arrest) (Month, Day)
(03) _____ (Date of birth) (04) _____ (Age) (05) _____ (Sex)	(10) _____ (Time of arrest)
(06) _____ (Occupation) (07) _____ (Where employed)	(11) _____ (Place of arrest)
(12) _____ (Specific offenses)	
(13) _____ (Arresting Officer)	(14) _____ (Officer's No.)

19. What entry should be made in Blank 01?

    A. Jo Ann Jones
    B. Jones, Jo Ann
    C. Mary Wiell
    D. Wiell, Mary A.

20. Which of the following should be entered in Blank 04?

    A. 40   B. 40's   C. 45   D. Middle-aged

21. Which of the following should be entered in Blank 09?

    A. Wednesday, February 1, 10:30 A.M.
    B. February 1
    C. Thursday morning, February 2
    D. Morning, February 4

22. Of the following, which would be the BEST entry to make in Blank 11?

    A. Really Street Welfare Center
    B. Brooklyn
    C. 435 E. Smythe St., Brooklyn
    D. 118 Healy St., Apt. 4F

Questions 23-27.

DIRECTIONS: Answer Questions 23 through 27 on the basis of the information given in the Report of Loss or Theft that appears below.

```
| REPORT OF LOSS OR THEFT              Date: 12/4     Time: 9:15 a.m. |
| Complaint made by:  Richard Aldridge          [ ] Owner             |
|                     306 S. Walter St.         [x] Other - explain:  |
|                                               Head of Accty. Dept.  |
```

Type of property: _Computer_   Value: _$550.00_
Description: _Dell_
Location: _768 N Margin Ave., Accounting Dept., 3rd Floor_
Time: _Overnight 12/3 - 12/4_
Circumstances: _Mr. Aldridge reports he arrived at work 8:45 A.M., found office door open and machine missing. Nothing else reported missing. I investigated and found signs of forced entry: door lock was broken._   Signature of Reporting Officer: _B.L. Ramirez_

Notify:
[ ] Building & Grounds Office, 768 N. Margin Ave.
[ ] Lost Property Office, 110 Brand Ave.
[x] Security Office, 703 N. Wide Street

23. The person who made this complaint is
    A. a secretary   B. a security officer
    C. Richard Aldridge   D. B.L. Ramirez

24. The report concerns a computer that has been
    A. lost   B. damaged   C. stolen   D. sold

25. The person who took the computer probably entered the office through
    A. a door   B. a window   C. the roof   D. the basement

26. When did the head of the Accounting Department first notice that the computer was missing?
    A. December 4 at 9:15 A.M.   B. December 4 at 8:45 A.M.
    C. The night of December 3   D. The night of December 4

27. The event described in the report took place at
    A. 306 South Walter Street   B. 768 North Margin Avenue
    C. 110 Brand Avenue   D. 703 North Wide Street

Questions 28-33.

DIRECTIONS: Answer Questions 28 through 33 on the basis of the instructions, the code, and the sample question given below.

Assume that a special officer (security officer) at a certain location is equipped with a two-way radio to keep him in constant touch with his security headquarters. Radio messages and replies are given in code form, as follows:

Radio Code for Situation	J	P	M	F	B
Radio Code for Action to be Taken	o	r	a	z	q
Radio Response for Action Being Taken	1	2	3	4	5

Assume that each of the above capital letters is the radio code for a particular type of situation, that the small letter below each capital letter is the radio code for the action a special officer (security officer) is directed to take, and that the number directly below each small letter is the radio response a special officer (security officer) should make to indicate what action was actually taken.

In each of the following Questions 28 through 33, the code letter for the action directed (Column 2) and the code number for the action taken (Column 3) should correspond to the capital letters in Column 1.

If only Column 2 is different from Column 1, mark your answer A.

If only Column 3 is different from Column 1, mark your answer B.

If both Column 2 and Column 3 are different from Column 1, mark your answer C.

If both Columns 2 and 3 are the same as Column 1, mark your answer D.

SAMPLE QUESTION

Column 1	Column 2	Column 3
JPFMB	orzaq	12453

The code letters in Column 2 are correct, but the numbers 53 in Column 3 should be 35. Therefore, the answer is B.

	Column 1	Column 2	Column 3	
28.	PBFJM	rqzoa	25413	28.____
29.	MPFBJ	zrqao	32541	29.____
30.	JBFPM	oqzra	15432	30.____
31.	BJPMF	qaroz	51234	31.____
32.	PJFMB	rozaq	21435	32.____
33.	FJBMP	zoqra	41532	33.____

Questions 34-40.

DIRECTIONS: Questions 34 through 40 are based on the instructions given below. Study the instructions and the sample question; then answer Questions 34 through 40 on the basis of this information

INSTRUCTIONS:

In each of the following Questions 34 through 40, the 3-line name and address in Column 1 is the master-list entry, and the 3-line entry in Column 2 is the information to be checked against the master list.

If there is one line that does not match, mark your answer A.

If there are two lines that do not match, mark your answer B.

If all three lines do not match, mark your answer C.

If the lines all match exactly, mark your answer D.

SAMPLE QUESTION:

Column 1
Mark L. Field
11-09 Prince Park Blvd.
Bronx, N.Y. 11402

Column 2
Mark L. Field
11-99 Prince Park
Bronx, N.Y. 11401

The first lines in each column match exactly. The second lines do not match, since 11-09 does not match 11-99 and Blvd. does not match Way. The third lines do not match either, since 11402 does not match 11401. Therefore, there are two lines that do not match and the correct answer is B.

	Column 1	Column 2	
34.	Jerome A. Jackson 1243 14th Avenue New York, N.Y. 10023	Jerome A. Johnson 1234 14th Avenue New York, N.Y. 10023	34.____
35.	Sophie Strachtheim 33-28 Connecticut Ave. Far Rockaway, N.Y. 11697	Sophie Strachtheim 33-28 Connecticut Ave. Far Rockaway, N.Y. 11697	35.____
36.	Elisabeth N.T. Gorrell 256 Exchange St. New York, N.Y. 10013	Elizabeth N.T. Gorrell 256 Exchange St. New York, N.Y. 10013	36.____
37.	Maria J. Gonzalez 7516 E. Sheepshead Rd. Brooklyn, N.Y. 11240	Maria J. Gonzalez 7516 N. Shepshead Rd. Brooklyn, N.Y. 11240	37.____
38.	Leslie B. Brautenweiler 21 57A Seller Terr. Flushing, N.Y. 11367	Leslie B. Brautenwieler 21-75A Seiler Terr. Flushing, N.J. 11367	38.____

10 (#2)

39. Rigoberto J. Peredes
    157 Twin Towers, #18F
    Tottenville, S.I., N.Y.

40. Pietro F. Albino
    P.O. Box 7548
    Floral Park, N.Y. 11005

Rigoberto J. Peredes
157 Twin Towers, #18F
Tottenville, S.I., N.Y.

Pietro F. Albina
P.O. Box 7458
Floral Park, N.Y. 11005

39. ____

40. ____

KEY (CORRECT ANSWERS)

1. D	11. A	21. B	31. A
2. C	12. D	22. C	32. D
3. B	13. C	23. C	33. A
4. D	14. B	24. C	34. B
5. B	15. A	25. A	35. D
6. A	16. C	26. B	36. A
7. C	17. C	27. B	37. A
8. D	18. C	28. D	38. C
9. D	19. D	29. C	39. D
10. D	20. C	30. B	40. B

EXAMINATION SECTION
TEST 1

DIRECTIONS: Each question or incomplete statement is followed by several suggested answers or completions. Select the one that BEST answers the question or completes the statement. *PRINT THE LETTER OF THE CORRECT ANSWER IN THE SPACE AT THE RIGHT.*

1. Which of the following is the LEAST important factor to consider in surveying the physical layout of a building for traffic flow? 1.____

    A. Location of windows
    B. Number of entrances
    C. Number of exits
    D. Location of first aid rooms

2. The major purpose of any security program in a large organization is to prevent unlawful acts. 2.____
   If adequate patrol coverage is provided at a given location, it is MOST likely that

    A. crimes will not be committed
    B. undesirables will not enter the building
    C. unlawful acts will increase in the long run
    D. there will be less opportunity to commit a crime

3. The MOST frequent cause of fires in public facilities is 3.____

    A. incinerators   B. vandalism
    C. electrical sources   D. smoking on the job

4. After bomb threats are received, it is sometimes necessary to evacuate a facility. How long BEFORE the threatened time of explosion should a facility be evacuated? 4.____
   At least _____ minutes.

    A. 15   B. 25   C. 50   D. 60

5. Once a facility is evacuated because of a bomb threat, how much time should pass before the public and employees are allowed to enter the building? 5.____
   _____ minutes.

    A. 10   B. 20   C. 40   D. 60

6. Of the following locations in public buildings, the one which is the LEAST likely place for bombs to be planted is in 6.____

    A. storerooms   B. bathrooms
    C. cafeterias   D. waste receptacles

7. The one of the following that is the surest means of establishing positive identification of someone entering a facility is by 7.____

    A. personal recognition   B. I.D. badge
    C. social security card   D. driver's license

8. The one of the following which most probably would NOT be included in a police record report concerning an incident at a facility is the

   A. name of complainant or injured party
   B. name of the investigating officer
   C. statement of each witness
   D. religion of complainant or injured party

9. Preventing trouble is one of the primary concerns of special officers.
   When dealing with unruly groups of people who threaten to become violent, which of the following is a measure which should NOT be taken?

   A. Maintain close surveillance of such groups
   B. Try to contact the leaders of the group regardless of their militancy
   C. Keep the officer force alerted
   D. Have the officer force deal aggressively with provocations

10. Of the following, the MOST important factor to consider in the deployment of officers dealing with a client population is the officers' ability to

    A. remain calm
    B. look stern
    C. evaluate personality
    D. take a firm stand

11. Assume that an offender is struggling with a group of officers who are trying to arrest him.
    What force, if any, can be used to overcome this resistance?

    A. The amount of force acceptable to the public
    B. The amount of force necessary to restrain the offender and protect the officers
    C. Any amount of force that is acceptable to the officers at the scene
    D. No force may be used until the police arrive

12. Assume that a fire is discovered at your work location. The one of the following actions which would be INAPPROPRIATE for you to take is to

    A. notify the telephone operator
    B. station a reliable person at the entrance
    C. open all windows and doors in the area
    D. start evacuating the area

13. If a person has an object caught in his throat or air passage but is breathing adequately, which one of the following should you do?

    A. Probe for the object
    B. Force him to drink water
    C. Lay him over your arm and slap him between the shoulder blades
    D. Allow him to cough and to assume the position he finds most comfortable

14. The one of the following methods which should NOT be used to report a fire is to

    A. call 911
    B. pull the handle in the red box on the street corner
    C. call the fire department county numbers listed in each county directory
    D. call 411

15. Assume that an officer, alone in a building at night, smells the strong odor of cooking or heating gas. In addition to airing the building and making sure that he is not overcome, it would be BEST for the officer to call

    A. his superior at his home and ask for instructions
    B. for a plumber from the department of public works
    C. 911 for police and fire help
    D. the emergency number at Con Edison

16. Of the following situations, the one that is MOST dangerous for an officer is when he

    A. investigates suspicious persons and circumstances
    B. finds a burglary in progress or pursues burglary suspects
    C. attempts an arrest or finds a robbery in progress
    D. patrols on the overnight shift

17. An officer on security patrol generally should spend MOST of his time

    A. checking doors and locks
    B. helping the public and answering questions
    C. chasing criminals and looking for clues
    D. writing reports on unusual incidents

18. The one of the following that is an ACCEPTABLE way to arrest a person is to

    A. tell him to report to the nearest police precinct
    B. send a summons to his permanent address
    C. tell him in person that he is under arrest
    D. show him handcuffs and ask him to come along

19. A carbon dioxide fire extinguisher is BEST suited for extinguishing _____ fires.

    A. paper   B. rag   C. rubbish   D. grease

20. A pressurized water or soda-acid fire extinguisher is BEST suited for extinguishing _____ fires.

    A. wood
    B. gasoline
    C. electrical
    D. magnesium

21. The one of the following statements that does NOT apply to the use of handcuffs is that they

    A. are used as temporary restraining devices
    B. eliminate the need for vigilance
    C. cannot be opened without keys
    D. are used to secure a violent person

22. The one of the following that is GENERALLY a crime against the person is

    A. trespass   B. burglary   C. robbery   D. arson

23. Of the following, the SAFEST way of escape from an office in a burning building is generally the

    A. stairway
    B. rooftop
    C. passenger elevator
    D. freight elevator

24. In attempting to control a possible riot situation, an officer pushed his way into a crowd gathered outside the building and tried to cause confusion by arguing with members of the group.
    This procedure NORMALLY is considered

    A. *desirable;* any violence that occurs will remain outside the building
    B. *desirable;* the crowd will break into smaller groups and disperse
    C. *undesirable;* to maintain control of the situation, the officer must not become part of the crowd
    D. *undesirable;* the supervisor should stay clear of the scene

25. Which one of the following is MOST effective in making officers more safety-minded?

    A. Maintaining an up-to-date library of the latest safety literature
    B. Reading daily safety bulletins at roll-call
    C. Holding informal group safety meetings periodically
    D. Offering prizes for good safety slogans and displays

KEY (CORRECT ANSWERS)

1. A	11. B
2. D	12. C
3. C	13. D
4. A	14. D
5. D	15. D
6. C	16. C
7. A	17. A
8. D	18. C
9. D	19. D
10. A	20. A

21. B
22. C
23. A
24. C
25. C

TEST 2

DIRECTIONS: Each question or incomplete statement is followed by several suggested answers or completions. Select the one that BEST answers the question or completes the statement. *PRINT THE LETTER OF THE CORRECT ANSWER IN THE SPACE AT THE RIGHT.*

1. Assume that an angry crowd of some 75 to 100 people has built up in one of the hallways of a center and that only one superior officer and two subordinate officers are on duty in the building. A glass panel in one of the stairway doors has just been broken under the pressure of the crowd and a bench has been hurled down a flight of stairs. The one of the following actions that the superior officer SHOULD take in this situation is to

    A. push his way into the crowd and try to reason with them
    B. order the two other officers to try to quiet the crowd
    C. call the police on 911 and meet them outside the building
    D. do nothing at this point in order to avoid a riot

2. One of the duties and responsibilities of a supervisor is to test the knowledge of the officers concerning their post conditions.
   This should be done if the officer's assignment is

    A. fixed only
    B. roving only
    C. roving only in a troublesome spot
    D. either fixed or roving

3. An officer discovers early one morning that an office in the building he guards has been burglarized.
   Of the following, it is important for the officer to FIRST

    A. go through the building and look for suspects
    B. call the police and protect the area and whatever evidence exists until they arrive
    C. allow people into their offices as they come to work
    D. examine, sort, and handle all evidence before the police get there

4. Assume that two officers are interrogating one suspect. How should these officers position themselves during the interrogation?

    A. One officer should stand on either side of the suspect.
    B. One officer should stand to the right of the suspect, and the other officer should stand behind the suspect.
    C. Both officers should stand to the right of the suspect.
    D. One officer should stand to the right of the suspect, and the other officer should stand in front of the suspect.

5. A witness who takes an oath to testify truly and who states as true any matter which he knows to be false is guilty of

    A. perjury   B. libel   C. slander   D. fraud

6. An officer checking a substance suspected of containing narcotics should GENERALLY

   A. taste it in small amounts
   B. send it to a laboratory for analysis
   C. smell it for its distinctive odor
   D. examine it for its unusual texture

7. A certain center is situated in an area where frequent outbreaks of hostilities seem to be focused on the center itself.
Which of the following BEST explains why the center may be a target for hostile acts?
It

   A. serves community needs
   B. represents governmental authority
   C. represents all ethnic groups
   D. serves as a neutral battlefield

8. An officer often deals with people who might be addicted to drugs.
The one of the following symptoms which is NOT generally an indication of drug addiction is

   A. dilation of the eye pupils
   B. frequent yawning and sneezing
   C. a deep, rasping cough
   D. continual itching of the arms and legs

9. In emergency situations, panic will MOST probably occur when people are

   A. unexpectedly confronted with a terrorizing condition from which there appears to be no escape
   B. angry and violent
   C. anxious about circumstances which are not obvious, easily visible or within the immediate area
   D. familiar with the effects of the emergency

10. The one of the following actions on the part of a person that would NOT be considered *resisting arrest* is

    A. retreating and running away
    B. saying, *You can't arrest me*
    C. pushing the officer aside
    D. pulling away from an officer's grasp

11. Which of the following items would NOT be considered an APPROPRIATE item of uniform for an officer to wear while on duty?

    A. Reefer type overcoat
    B. Leather laced shoes with flat soles
    C. White socks
    D. Cap cover with cap device displayed

12. What can happen to an officer if the leather thong on his night stick is NOT twisted correctly?
The

   A. baton may be taken out of the officer's hand
   B. officer's wrist may be broken
   C. leather will tear more easily
   D. officer's arm may be injured

13. The one of the following kinds of information which SHOULD be included in the log book is

   A. any important matter of police information
   B. an item noted in Standard Operating Procedures only
   C. everything of general interest
   D. a crime or offense only

14. While on patrol at your work location, you receive a call that an assault has taken place. Upon your arrival at the scene, the victim, who has severe lacerations, informs you that the assailant ran into a nearby basement.
After apprehending the suspect, the type of search you should conduct is a _____ search.

   A. wall   B. frisk   C. body   D. strip

15. A tactical force is valuable in MOST emergency situations PRIMARILY because of its

   A. location
   B. morale
   C. flexibility
   D. size

16. An officer should be encouraged to talk easily and frankly when he is dealing with his superior.
In order to encourage such free communication, it would be MOST appropriate for a superior to behave in a(n)

   A. *sincere* manner; assure the officer that you will deal with him honestly and openly
   B. *official* manner; you are a superior officer and must always act formally with subordinates
   C. *investigative* manner; you must probe and question to get to a basis of trust
   D. *unemotional* manner; the officer's emotions and background should play no part in your dealings with him

17. Research findings show that an increase in free communication within an agency GENERALLY results in which one of the following?

   A. Improved morale and productivity
   B. Increased promotional opportunities
   C. An increase in authority
   D. A spirit of honesty

18. Assume that you are a superior officer and your superiors have given you a new arrest procedure to be followed. Before passing this information on to your subordinates, the one of the following actions that you should take FIRST is to

    A. ask your superiors to send out a memorandum to the entire staff
    B. clarify the procedure in your own mind
    C. set up a training course to provide instructions on the new procedure
    D. write a memorandum to your subordinates

19. Communication is necessary for an organization to be effective.
    The one of the following which is LEAST important for most communication systems is that

    A. messages are sent quickly and directly to the person who needs them to operate
    B. information should be conveyed understandably and accurately
    C. the method used to transmit information should be kept secret so that security can be maintained
    D. senders of messages must know how their messages were received and acted upon

20. Which one of the following is the CHIEF advantage of listening willingly to subordinate officers and encouraging them to talk freely and honestly?
    It

    A. reveals to superiors the degree to which ideas that are passed down are accepted by subordinates
    B. reduces the participation of subordinates in the operation of the department
    C. encourages officers to try for promotion
    D. enables officers to learn about security leaks on the part of officials

21. A superior may be informed through either oral or written reports.
    Which one of the following is an ADVANTAGE of using oral reports?

    A. There is no need for a formal record of the report.
    B. An exact duplicate of the report is not easily transmitted to others.
    C. A good oral report requires little time for preparation.
    D. An oral report involves two-way communication between a subordinate and his superior.

22. Of the following, the MOST important reason why officers should communicate effectively with the public is to

    A. improve the public's understanding of information that is important for them to know
    B. establish a friendly relationship
    C. obtain information about the kinds of people who come to the center
    D. convince the public that services are adequate

23. Officers should generally NOT use phrases like *too hard, too easy,* and *a lot* principally because such phrases

    A. may be offensive to some minority groups
    B. are too informal

C. mean different things to different people
D. are difficult to remember

24. The ability to communicate clearly and concisely is an important element in effective leadership. 24.____
Which of the following statements about oral and written communication is GENERALLY true?

   A. Oral communication is more time-consuming.
   B. Written communication is more likely to be misinterpreted.
   C. Oral communication is useful only in emergencies.
   D. Written communication is useful mainly when giving information to fewer than twenty people.

25. Rumors can often have harmful and disruptive effects on an organization. 25.____
Which one of the following is the BEST way to prevent rumors from becoming a problem?

   A. Refuse to act on rumors, thereby making them less believable
   B. Increase the amount of information passed along by the *grapevine*
   C. Distribute as much factual information as possible
   D. Provide training in report writing

KEY (CORRECT ANSWERS)

1.	C	11.	C
2.	D	12.	A
3.	B	13.	A
4.	B	14.	A
5.	A	15.	C
6.	B	16.	A
7.	B	17.	A
8.	C	18.	B
9.	A	19.	C
10.	B	20.	A

21. D
22. A
23. C
24. B
25. C

EXAMINATION SECTION
TEST 1

DIRECTIONS: Questions 1 through 5 are to be answered on the basis of the information, instructions, and sample question given below. Each question contains a GENERAL RULE, EXCEPTIONS, a PROBLEM, and the ACTION actually taken.

The GENERAL RULE explains what the special officer (security officer) should or should not do.

The EXCEPTIONS describe circumstances under which a special officer (security officer) should take action contrary to the GENERAL RULE.

However, an unusual emergency may justify taking an action that is not covered either by the GENERAL RULE or by the stated EXCEPTIONS.

The PROBLEM describes a situation requiring some action by the special officer (security officer).

ACTION describes what a special officer (security officer) actually did in that particular case.

Read carefully the GENERAL RULE and EXCEPTIONS, the PROBLEM, and the ACTION, and the mark A, B, C, or D in the space at the right in accordance with the following instructions:

I. If an action is clearly justified under the general rule, mark your answer A.
II. If an action is not justified under the general rule, but is justified under a stated exception, mark your answer B.
III. If an action is not justified either by the general rule or by a stated exception, but does seem strongly justified by an unusual emergency situation, mark your answer C.
IV. If an action does not seem justified for any of these reasons, mark your answer D.

SAMPLE QUESTION:

GENERAL RULE: A special officer (security officer) is not empowered to stop a person and search him for hidden weapons.
EXCEPTION: He may stop a person and search him if he has good reason to believe that he may be carrying a hidden weapon. Good reasons to believe he may be carrying a hidden weapon include (a) notification through official channels that a person may be armed, (b) a statement directly to the special officer (security officer) by the person himself that he is armed, and (c) the special officer's (security officer's) own direct observation.

PROBLEM: A special officer (security officer) on duty at a hospital clinic is notified by a woman patient at the clinic that a man sitting near her is making muttered threats that he has a gun and is going to shoot his doctor if the doctor gives him any trouble. Although the woman is upset, she seems to be telling the truth, and two other waiting patients con-

firm this. However, the special officer (security officer) approaches the man and sees no sign of a hidden weapon. The man tells the officer that he has no weapon.
ACTION: The special officer (security officer) takes the man aside into an empty office and proceeds to frisk him for a concealed weapon.

ANSWER: The answer cannot be A, because the general rule is that a special officer (security officer) is not empowered to search a person for hidden weapons. The answer cannot be B, because the notification did not come through official channels, the man did not tell the special officer (security officer) that he had a weapon, and the special officer (security officer) did not observe any weapon. However, since three people have confirmed that the man has said he has a weapon and is threatening to use it, this is pretty clearly an emergency situation that calls for action. Therefore, the answer is C.

1. GENERAL RULE: A special officer (security officer) on duty at a certain entrance is not to leave his post unguarded at any time.
EXCEPTION: He may leave the post for a brief period if he first summons a replacement. He may also leave if it is necessary for him to take prompt emergency action to prevent injury to persons or property.
PROBLEM: The special officer (security officer) sees a man running down a hall with a piece of iron pipe in his hand, chasing another man who is shouting for help. By going in immediate pursuit, there is a good chance that the special officer (security officer) can stop the man with the pipe.
ACTION: The special officer (security officer) leaves his post unguarded and pursues the man.

   The CORRECT answer is:

   A. I B. II C. III D. IV

2. GENERAL RULE: Special officers (security officers) assigned to a college campus are instructed not to arrest students for minor violations such as disorderly conduct; instead, the violation should be stopped and the incident should be reported to the college authorities, who will take disciplinary action.
EXCEPTION: A special officer (security officer) may arrest a student or take other appropriate action if failure to do so is likely to result in personal injury or property damage, or disruption of school activities, or if the incident involves serious criminal behavior.
PROBLEM: A special officer (security officer) is on duty in a college building where evening classes are being held. He is told that two students are causing a disturbance in a classroom. He arrives and finds that a fist fight is in progress and the classroom is in an uproar. The special officer (security officer) separates the two students who are fighting and takes them out of the room. Both of them seem to be intoxicated. They both have valid student ID cards.
ACTION: The special officer (security officer) takes down their names and addresses for his report, then tells them to leave the building with a warning not to return this evening.

   The CORRECT answer is:

   A. I B. II C. III D. IV

3. GENERAL RULE: A special officer (security officer) is not permitted to carry a gun while on duty.
EXCEPTION: A special officer (security officer) who disarms a person must keep the weapon in his possession for the brief period before he can turn it over to the proper authorities. A special officer (security officer) who is NOT on duty may, like any other citizen, own and carry a gun if he has a proper permit from the Police Department.
PROBLEM: A special officer (security officer) is assigned to a post where there have been a series of violent incidents in the past few days. He feels that these incidents could have been controlled much more easily if the people involved had seen that the special officer (security officer) had a gun. He has a gun at home, for which he has a valid permit.
ACTION: The special officer (security officer) brings his gun when he goes on duty. He does not plan to use it, but just show people that he has it so that they will not start any trouble.

The CORRECT answer is:

A. I B. II C. III D. IV

4. GENERAL RULE: No one except a licensed physician or someone acting directly under a physician's orders may legally administer medicine to another person.
EXCEPTION: In a first aid situation, the special officer (security officer) is allowed to help a person suffering frori a heart condition or other disease to take medicine which the person has in his possession, provided that the person is conscious and requests this assistance.
PROBLEM: A special officer (security officer) on duty at a public building is told that a man has collapsed in the elevator. When the special officer (security officer) arrives at the scene, the man is barely conscious. He cannot speak, but he points to his pocket. The special officer (security officer) finds a pill bottle that says *one capsule in ease of need*. The man nods.
ACTION: The special officer (security officer) puts one capsule in the man's hand and guides the man's hand to his mouth.

The CORRECT answer is:

A. I B. II C. III D. IV

5. GENERAL RULE: In case of a fire drill or fire alarm, special officers (security officers) on patrol in a building are to remain in their assigned areas to assist in the evacuation of persons from the building and to make sure that no one takes advantage of the situation by stealing property that is left unguarded.
EXCEPTION: Should there be an actual fire, special officers (security officers) will follow whatever instructions are given by the firefighters or police officers who arrive on the scene to take charge.
PROBLEM: A special officer (security officer) is on duty patroling the fifth floor of a building when a fire alarm sounds. The fire is in a supply closet at one end of the fifth floor. All personnel have been evacuated from the floor. Neither police nor firemen have yet shown up.
ACTION: The special officer (security officer) stays on the fifth floor at a safe distance from the supply closet.

The CORRECT answer is:

A. I B. II C. III D. IV

KEY (CORRECT ANSWERS)

1. B
2. A
3. D
4. B
5. A

———

EXAMINATION SECTION
TEST 1

DIRECTIONS: Each question or incomplete statement is followed by several suggested answers or completions. Select the one that BEST answers the question or completes the statement. *PRINT THE LETTER OF THE CORRECT ANSWER IN THE SPACE AT THE RIGHT.*

1. As a general rule, which of the following areas on a campus would be most in need of protection by a physical barrier?
   Areas

   A. set aside for group activities
   B. smaller than 40 feet in diameter
   C. with roof access
   D. less than 18 feet above ground

2. For a campus officer to be armed, it is customary for him to complete a signed statement pledging himself to certain guidelines. Which of the following would typically be included in such a statement?
   I. The firearm will never be used as a club or similar weapon.
   II. Before shooting directly at a person, the officer will fire at least one warning shot.
   III. The firearm is only to be drawn when the officer's life, or the life of another, is threatened.
   IV. Shots directed at a perpetrator should be intended to disable, rather than kill.
   The CORRECT answer is:

   A. I, III
   B. I, III, IV
   C. III *only*
   D. II, III, IV

3. An arrest that is made after the security officer sees the offense committed is known as an arrest on

   A. reasonable suspicion of probable cause
   B. view
   C. detention
   D. complaint

4. The gate valve alarm of a sprinkler system has sounded. This means that the

   A. sprinkler system has been activated
   B. main water riser to the valve has been shut off
   C. storage water level has dropped below minimum requirements
   D. secondary water valve has been closed

5. A *dry* fire — from burning wood, paper, or textiles — is classified as Class

   A. A   B. B   C. C   D. D

6. The main DISADVANTAGE associated with the use of local alarms in security systems is that

    A. sometimes nobody is around to hear them
    B. they are dependent on electrical power
    C. they must be placed in multiple locations
    D. they don't deter criminals from breaking and entering

7. Each of the following is a symptom exhibited by *huffers* of vapors produced by glue, gasoline, paint, or other substances EXCEPT

    A. slurred speech   B. violent behavior
    C. coughing   D. increased appetite

8. Legally, a theft from the inside of a vehicle that has been locked and entered unlawfully is called

    A. robbery   B. grand larceny
    C. burglary   D. petty larceny

9. Security problems that may be caused by severe heat include

    A. increased likelihood of loss of power
    B. electrical overheating
    C. greater ability for people to hide stolen property
    D. increased likelihood of fires

10. Which of the following campus features does the most to necessitate a 24-hour radio dispatcher?

    A. residential community
    B. contractual installation such as food service
    C. valuable collection
    D. high-rise building or buildings

11. If rounds clocks are used by an officer on patrol,

    A. the clock areas should be evenly spaced
    B. each clock must be punched on every round, regardless of the order
    C. the clock locations should never be changed
    D. they should be punched in exactly the same order each time

12. Because of the operating costs involved, a _____ alarm system is used primarily for government-owned facilities.

    A. remote   B. central station
    C. local   D. proprietary station

13. When assisting victims at the scene of an accident, an officer may
    I. give nonprescription medication
    II. restrain a person who is having a seizure
    III. treat a victim for shock
    IV. give the person fluids if the person is conscious
    The CORRECT answer is:

    A. I only   B. II only   C. III, IV   D. IV only

14. When a(n) _____ is NOT generally an occasion on which a person, automobile, or premises may be legally searched.

    A. subject is being held for questioning
    B. warrant has been obtained
    C. emergency situation exists
    D. lawful arrest has been made

15. After a crime has been committed, a(n) _____ makes the most useful interview subject.

    A. witness   B. victim   C. suspect   D. informant

16. A _____ lock generally offers the LEAST amount of security.

    A. combination   B. pin tumbler
    C. disc tumbler   D. cipher

17. Evacuation guidelines for most campus buildings provide for an area warden, stair guard, and a group leader who is appointed from among the building's management personnel. Typically, a group leader will be responsible for controlling and directing about _____ people, depending on the floor size and layout.

    A. 5   B. 15   C. 25   D. 35

18. The campus has just received a bomb threat, and a search is underway. When searching individual rooms, an officer should begin

    A. at the door and move in a circular path
    B. at the corners and move inward
    C. with the furniture and then check the fixtures
    D. at the ceiling and move to the floor

19. The highest percentage of crime on school campuses typically occurs in

    A. classrooms and private offices
    B. residence hall or dorms
    C. parking lots
    D. commercial installations such as bookstores and food service

20. For most security applications, a report listing the holder of keys must be filed

    A. twice daily   B. daily
    C. twice weekly   D. weekly

21. The best driving speed for vehicle patrol services is generally between _____ miles per hour.

    A. 5-10   B. 15-20   C. 25-30   D. 35-40

22. Which of the following statements is generally FALSE?

    A. An officer should never approach a group of people without requesting backup, even if it is not needed.
    B. The officer should never draw a weapon as a tactic for discouraging violence.
    C. An officer should never confront hostile persons alone.
    D. When using a flashlight, the officer should hold it sheltered close to his body.

23. In general, security personnel may make an arrest if they
    I. observe a suspect taking property
    II. know a felony has been committed but did not see it happen
    III. know a misdemeanor has been committed but did not see it happen
    The CORRECT answer is:

    A. I only   B. I, II   C. I, III   D. II, III

24. Which of the following may be a visible symptom of the abuse of opiates such as morphine, codeine, or heroin?

    A. Antisocial behavior   B. Constricted eye functions
    C. Pale, sweaty skin   D. Rapid speech

25. A security officer is the first to arrive at the scene of an accident that has caused injury. The victim has an open wound that is bleeding dark red, in a steady stream. After taking precautions against blood-borne disease, the officer should

    A. flush the wound with water
    B. apply a tourniquet
    C. apply antiseptic
    D. apply direct pressure to the wound

26. When approaching a subject for a weapons search, the officer should inform the subject that the search is to be conducted

    A. after the subject has been apprehended
    B. from behind, with one hand placed on the subject's shoulder
    C. from the patrol car, through a bullhorn or intercom
    D. from a safe distance of at least five feet

27. Which of the following elements should be included in a shift report?
    I. Detailed accounts of reported incidents
    II. Time and number of patrol rounds completed
    III. Information on condition of lighting
    IV. Weather conditions
    The CORRECT answer is:

    A. I only   B. II, III, IV
    C. III, IV   D. I, II

28. A(n) _____ internal alarm would probably be most effective in protecting a safe or vault.

    A. audio   B. ultrasonic
    C. photoelectric   D. capacitance

29. A call has come in from a passenger on a stranded elevator to the switchboard operator. After the operator receives the relevant information, security and maintenance personnel are contacted. Security personnel should report to the

    A. floor where the elevator is stranded
    B. maintenance personnel for direction
    C. bottom floor
    D. top floor

30. The post indicator alarm of a sprinkler system has sounded. This means the

    A. sprinkler system has been activated
    B. main water riser to the valve has been shut off
    C. storage water level has dropped below minimum requirements
    D. secondary water valve has been closed

31. The primary goal of a private security officer at the scene of a recent crime is

    A. containment   B. witness interviews
    C. suspect apprehension   D. evidence gathering

32. If a security officer encounters an accident victim who has gone into shock, the officer should do each of the following EXCEPT

    A. keep the victim warm
    B. raise the victim's head
    C. treat injuries
    D. loosen the victim's clothing

33. For a security officer, the foundation of good report writing is considered to be

    A. through patrolling   B. good interviewing
    C. field note taking   D. outlining skills

34. The fundamental difference between a crime called *malicious destruction of property* and one called *vandalism* is one of

    A. jurisdiction
    B. apparent motive
    C. the monetary amount of damage
    D. the type of property that was damaged

35. The most commonly used form of access control in setting such as college campuses is

    A. cipher locks   B. compartmentalization
    C. flood lighting   D. entry gate posts

36. The _____ should be allowed input into the decision to arm security personnel for specific situations or events.
    I. employers of security personnel
    II. public
    III. security agency
    IV. local law enforcement agency
    The CORRECT answer is:

    A. I, III   B. I, IV
    C. II, III, IV   D. II, IV

37. Which of the following activities generally offers the greatest degree of flexibility in the delivery of security services?

    A. Report writing   B. Vehicle patrol
    C. Access control   D. Foot patrol

38. Which of the following is NOT a security concern that is generally associated with flooding?

   A. Usefulness of parking areas
   B. Evacuation plans
   C. Bursting water pipes
   D. Looting

39. Which of the following is a use-of-force guideline for private security personnel?

   A. If equipment (such as a flashlight) is not designed for use as a weapon, it should never be used for that purpose.
   B. If necessary, use a weapon as a form of intimidation to forestall the necessity of having to use it.
   C. Saps or billyclubs should be displayed prominently on the officer's belt to discourage resistance.
   D. The officer should use whatever force is necessary to overcome perceived resistance.

40. An informant has come forward to offer information about a crime that has been committed on campus. The security officer believes it is important to understand the informant's motivation for coming forward.
   Generally, the officer should approach this subject

   A. at the beginning of the interview
   B. when the informant least expects it
   C. after the informant has given an account, but before the officer has asked any questions
   D. at the conclusion of the interview

KEY (CORRECT ANSWERS)

1. D	11. A	21. B	31. A
2. A	12. A	22. D	32. B
3. B	13. C	23. B	33. C
4. D	14. A	24. B	34. B
5. A	15. A	25. D	35. D
6. A	16. C	26. D	36. A
7. D	17. B	27. B	37. B
8. C	18. A	28. D	38. C
9. D	19. B	29. A	39. A
10. A	20. B	30. B	40. D

TEST 2

DIRECTIONS: Each question or incomplete statement is followed by several suggested answers or completions. Select the one that BEST answers the question or completes the statement. *PRINT THE LETTER OF THE CORRECT ANSWER IN THE SPACE AT THE RIGHT.*

1. The campus has just received a bomb threat, and a search is underway. When searching individual rooms, team members should be instructed to

   A. start the search in the center of the room and move outward from there
   B. search slowly, first searching the area from the floor to waist height
   C. place a marker on any suspicious looking item
   D. enter a room completely before beginning the search

   1._____

2. When on a foot patrol assignment, an officer should

   A. turn the lights off whenever leaving a building
   B. stick to the shadows and avoid being seen
   C. observe the area to be patrolled before entering
   D. stick to the same pattern of patrolling

   2._____

3. Chemical fires are classified as Class

   A. A   B. B   C. C   D. D

   3._____

4. If campus security officers are to be armed, a _____ is typically most appropriate for their use.

   A. shotgun
   B. short-nosed .38-caliber revolver
   C. carbine
   D. long-nosed .357 magnum

   4._____

5. Which of the following is NOT a guideline that should be followed by security personnel who are on foot patrol at night?

   A. Avoid being lit from the back
   B. View the area to be patrolled in advance, if possible
   C. When entering buildings and are moving from room to room, open doors as quietly as possible
   D. Keep the flashlight on thumb pressure only

   5._____

6. Which of the following types of locks is most likely to be used with cabinets and desks?

   A. Combination lock   B. Disc tumbler lock
   C. Padlock   D. Cipher lock

   6._____

7. When on patrol, security personnel have an obligation to report
       I. traffic patterns
       II. improper employee conduct
       III. observed hazards
       IV. poor housekeeping or maintenance practices
   The CORRECT answer is:

   A. I *only*   B. II, IV
   C. II, III, IV   D. III, IV

   7._____

8. Towing policies for the enforcement of campus parking should include each of the following EXCEPT

   A. a contractual arrangement with a tow truck operator
   B. fines returnable to the local municipality, if possible
   C. the presence of a security officer at each towing incident
   D. a random pattern of towing that includes first-time offenders

9. Which of the following statements is generally TRUE?

   A. An officer should always display his badge prominently, especially when on night patrol.
   B. An officer should communicate with a dispatcher or other officers constantly while on duty.
   C. When approaching a vehicle, an officer should walk directly in front of the vehicle headlights.
   D. If a door has a window, an officer should look through it and examine the room before entering.

10. Which of the following is a sign that might be exhibited by a person who is on amphetamines or *uppers*?

    A. Loss of appetite
    B. Constricted pupils
    C. Rapid speech
    D. Uncontrolled laughing

11. Whenever possible, security policy guidelines for campus residence halls should include each of the following EXCEPT

    A. a periphery of high-intensity light around the exterior
    B. the use of interchangeable-core locking cylinders
    C. the use of only one main ground-floor entrance per building
    D. planting shrubs/trees outside first-floor rooms

12. An alarm system whose monitors are located in the main guard office is known as a _____ alarm system.

    A. remote
    B. central station
    C. local
    D. proprietary station

13. A security officer comes across a victim who has been badly burned. The officer should

    A. treat the victim for shock
    B. bandage the burn
    C. apply cold water to the burn
    D. apply an ointment or salve

14. Which of the following interview subjects typically presents a security officer with the least amount of difficulty?
    A(n)

    A. witness   B. victim   C. suspect   D. informant

15. Access control to any campus will be ineffective in any case if _____ are not provided.

    A. physical barriers
    B. weapons
    C. floodlights
    D. secure locks

16. Generally, security personnel may detain a person if
    I. it is known that the subject has information regarding a crime
    II. there is probable cause to believe the person has unlawfully taken property that can be recovered by holding the person for a reasonable period of time
    III. it is suspected that the person will commit a crime in the near future
    The CORRECT answer is:

    A. I, II   B. II only   C. III only   D. I, III

17. In general, departmental record control should place a _____ day limit on the time allotted for the removal of files from the office by security personnel.

    A. 1   B. 2-3   C. 5-7   D. 10-15

18. Keys to gates, buildings, and other secured equipment must generally be issued and returned by officers

    A. every day   B. every week
    C. every month   D. annually

19. A crime has just been committed and a security officer is the first to arrive at the scene. Before the police arrive, a handful of campus officials arrive and request to enter the crime scene.
    The best way to handle this is to

    A. keep them out by any means necessary
    B. request their cooperation in remaining outside the scene until the police have arrived
    C. refer them to the security supervisor
    D. defer to their wishes

20. Which of the following phrases has a different meaning from the others?

    A. Incident report   B. Post journal
    C. Shift report   D. Post log

21. In order to be effective, combination locks used for access control should have AT LEAST _____ numbers.

    A. 3   B. 4   C. 5   D. 6

22. The simplest, most effective, and trouble-free peripheral alarm system for low-risk applications would probably involve

    A. magnetic switches   B. button switches
    C. metallic foil tape D. audio switches

23. During a bomb search, a suspicious-looking package is found. Security personnel should

    A. move the package to a secure location
    B. place the package in water
    C. prevent anyone from touching the package
    D. place a tag on the package

24. When assisting a victim at the scene of an accident, an officer may
    I. describe an injury to the victim
    II. lift an injured person to a sitting position
    III. try to remove a foreign object from the victim's eye
    IV. attempt to keep the victim warm
    The CORRECT answer is:

    A. I only   B. II, III   C. IV only   D. III, IV

25. Each of the following is a symptom of shock EXCEPT

    A. slow pulse
    B. intense thirst
    C. dilated pupils
    D. irregular breathing

26. When on vehicle patrol, an officer should

    A. park directly in front of the building to be inspected
    B. observe from a distance or in a drive-by before driving into an area
    C. use spotlights to meet inspection requirements
    D. keep all windows closed while driving

27. Which of the following is a guideline to be followed by security personnel who are required to testify in court?

    A. Avoid asking attorneys to repeat their questions
    B. Never use the phrase *I think*
    C. Answer all questions as completely as possible
    D. Avoid looking directly at the judge or jury

28. Of the following types of arrest, the one that is most troublesome for security officers to justify is one that is made on

    A. reasonable suspicion of probable cause
    B. view
    C. detention
    D. complaint

29. The primary DISADVANTAGE associated with the use of central station alarm monitors is that

    A. time is lost from the time the signal is received until personnel arrive at the alarm area
    B. they do not provide a link to outside law enforcement agencies
    C. intruders are tipped off that the alarm has been activated
    D. they do not pin down the exact location of the alarm site

30. When writing any report, a security officer should

    A. write in the third person
    B. make sure there is at least one copy made
    C. use a formal outline
    D. use as few words as possible

31. Generally, campus property such as audio-visual equipment and office machinery should be inventoried at LEAST

    A. monthly
    B. quarterly
    C. annually
    D. every two years

32. Security personnel who carry firearms should generally be required to requalify themselves at a firing range every

    A. 4 months
    B. 6 months
    C. year
    D. two years

33. Which of the following campus building areas is generally LEAST likely to be used for the placement of a bomb?

    A. Elevator shafts
    B. Toilets
    C. Roofs
    D. Electrical panels

34. If padlocks are used in security systems, it is recommended that they be made of

    A. aluminum
    B. case-hardened steel
    C. cast iron
    D. hardened steel

35. An officer should make certain assumptions about foot patrol assignments. Which of the following is NOT one of these?

    A. Some form of communication is available for the officer to obtain assistance or request instructions.
    B. Most foot patrol assignments are single-officer duties.
    C. Only buildings that are open for public access will be included in the assignment.
    D. Back-up officers are available but are at some distance.

36. Which of the following statements about security personnel arrests is/are generally TRUE?
    I. The subject does not have to be under control in order for there to be an arrest.
    II. Detaining a person is a technical arrest.
    III. An arrest is made with the arresting persons identifying themselves and make a statement such as *you are under arrest,* and either touch the suspect or the suspect agrees.
    IV. The authority for the arrest must be known by the suspect.
    The CORRECT answer is:

    A. I, II, IV
    B. II, III, IV
    C. III, IV
    D. I, III

37. As a general rule, an area that is less than _____ from another structure should be protected by a physical barrier.

    A. 14 feet
    B. 25 feet
    C. 64 feet
    D. 100 yards

38. Security concerns associated with extreme cold include each of the following EXCEPT

    A. delayed communication
    B. physical danger from frozen surfaces
    C. increased opportunity for concealing objects under clothes
    D. integrity of plumbing systems

39. Fires from flammable liquids or grease are classified as Class 39.___

    A. A   B. B   C. C   D. D

40. When interviewing the victim of a crime, which of the following is a guideline that should generally be followed by a security officer? 40.___

    A. Make sure at least one other officer is present.
    B. Maintain a calm, steady demeanor.
    C. Get the facts by any means necessary.
    D. Keep the victim away from others who are familiar to him/her.

KEY (CORRECT ANSWERS)

1. B	11. D	21. B	31. C
2. C	12. D	22. A	32. A
3. D	13. A	23. C	33. C
4. B	14. D	24. C	34. D
5. C	15. A	25. A	35. C
6. B	16. B	26. B	36. B
7. C	17. B	27. B	37. A
8. D	18. A	28. A	38. A
9. B	19. B	29. A	39. B
10. C	20. A	30. B	40. B

MAP READING EXAMINATION SECTION
TEST 1

DIRECTIONS: Each question or incomplete statement is followed by several suggested answers or completions. Select the one that BEST answers the question or completes the Statement. *PRINT THE LETTER OF THE CORRECT ANSWER IN THE SPACE AT THE RIGHT.*

Questions 1-5.

DIRECTIONS: Questions 1 through 5 are to be answered SOLELY on the basis of the following information and map.

An employee may be required to assist civilians who seek travel directions or referral to city agencies and facilities.

The following is a map of part of a city, where several public offices and other institutions are located. Each of the squares represents one city block. Street names are as shown. If there is an arrow next to the street name, it means the street is one-way only in the direction of the arrow. If there is no arrow next to the street name, two-way traffic is allowed.

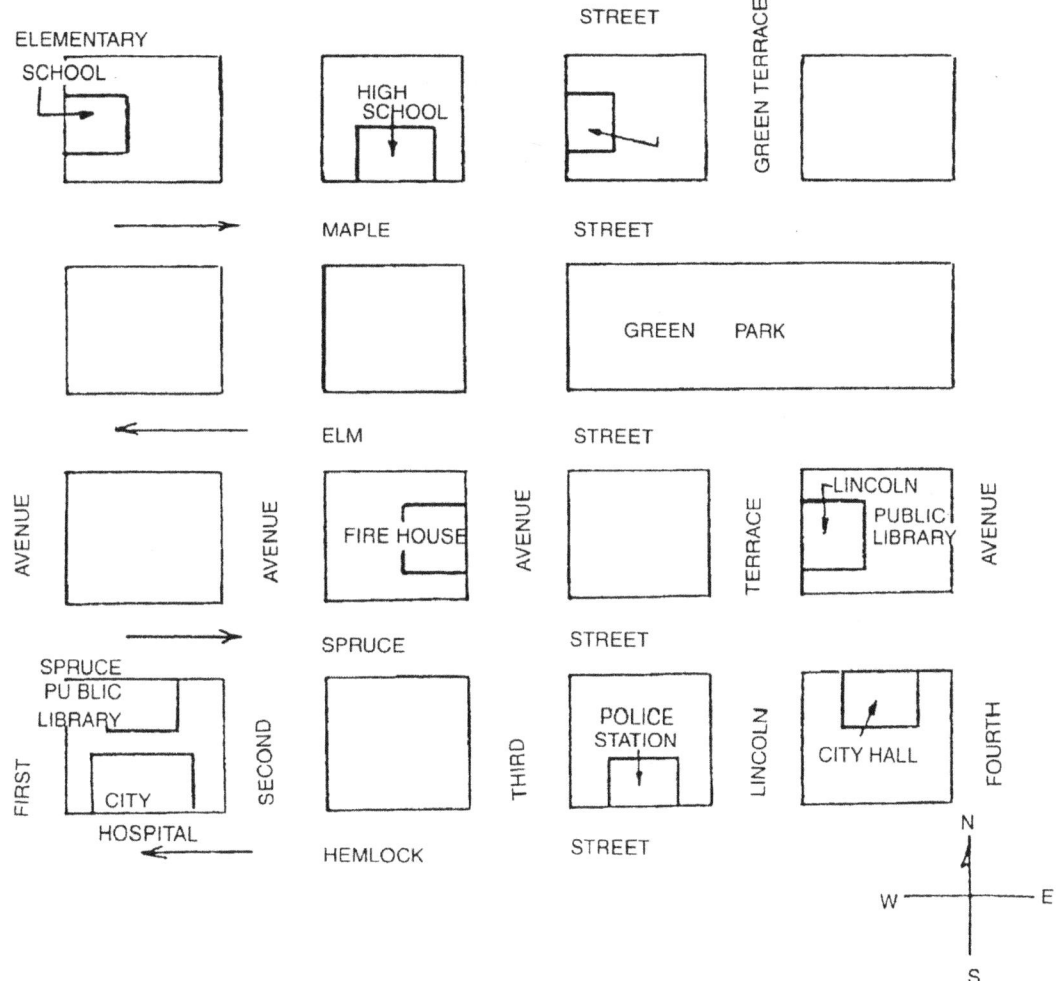

1. A woman whose handbag was stolen from her in Green Park asks a firefighter at the firehouse where to go to report the crime.
   The firefighter should tell the woman to go to the

   A. police station on Spruce Street
   B. police station on Hemlock Street
   C. city hall on Spruce Street
   D. city hall on Hemlock Street

1._____

2. A disabled senior citizen who lives on Green Terrace telephones the firehouse to ask which library is closest to her home.
   The firefighter should tell the senior citizen it is the

   A. Spruce Public Library on Lincoln Terrace
   B. Lincoln Public Library on Spruce Street
   C. Spruce Public Library on Spruce Street
   D. Lincoln Public Library on Lincoln Terrace

2._____

3. A woman calls the firehouse to ask for the exact location of City Hall.
   She should be told that it is on

   A. Hemlock Street, between Lincoln Terrace and Fourth Avenue
   B. Spruce Street, between Lincoln Terrace and Fourth Avenue
   C. Lincoln Terrace, between Spruce Street and Elm Street
   D. Green Terrace, between Maple Street and Pine Street

3._____

4. A delivery truck driver is having trouble finding the high school to make a delivery. The driver parks the truck across from the firehouse on Third Avenue facing north and goes into the firehouse to ask directions.
   In giving directions, the firefighter should tell the driver to go _____ to the school.

   A. north on Third Avenue to Pine Street and then make a right
   B. south on Third Avenue, make a left on Hemlock Street, and then make a right on Second Avenue
   C. north on Third Avenue, turn left on Elm Street, make a right on Second Avenue and go to Maple Street, then make another right
   D. north on Third Avenue to Maple Street, and then make a left

4._____

5. A man comes to the firehouse accompanied by his son and daughter. He wants to register his son in the high school and his daughter in the elementary school. He asks a firefighter which school is closest for him to walk to from the firehouse.
   The firefighter should tell the man that the

   A. high school is closer than the elementary school
   B. elementary school is closer than the high school
   C. elementary school and high school are the same distance away
   D. elementary school and high school are in opposite directions

5._____

Questions 6-8.

DIRECTIONS: Questions 6 through 8 are to be answered SOLELY on the basis of the following map and information. The flow of traffic is indicated by the arrows. If there is only one arrow shown, then traffic flows in the direction indicated by the arrow. If there are two arrows, then traffic flows in both directions. You must follow the flow of traffic

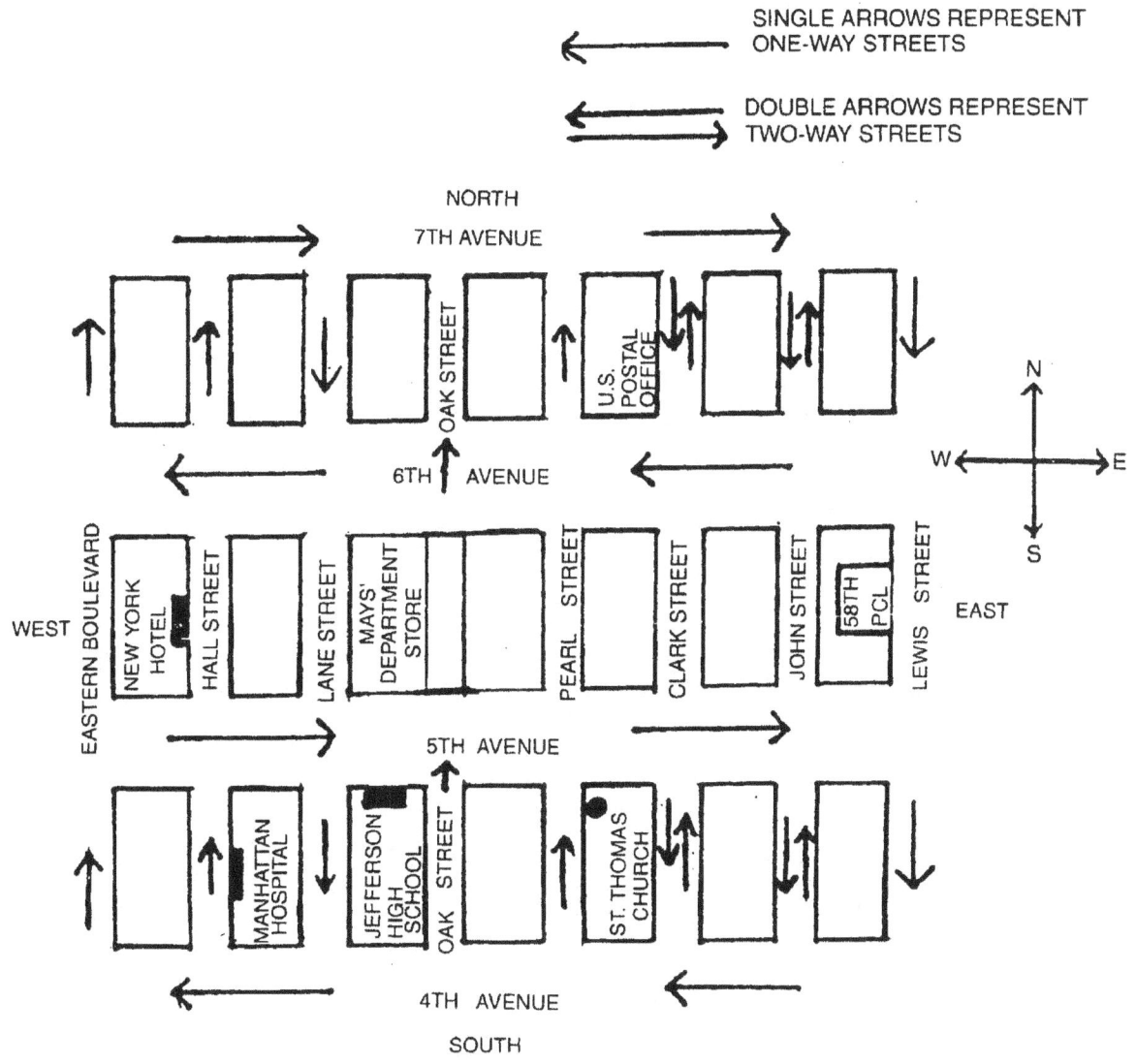

6. Traffic Enforcement Agent Fox was on foot patrol at John Street between 6th and 7th Avenues when a motorist driving southbound asked her for directions to the New York Hotel, which is located on Hall Street between 5th and 6th Avenues. Which one of the following is the SHORTEST route for Agent Fox to direct the motorist to take, making sure to obey all traffic regulations?
Travel _____ to the New York Hotel.

   A. north on John Street, then east on 7th Avenue, then north on Lewis Street, then west on 4th Avenue, then north on Eastern Boulevard, then east on 5th Avenue, then north on Hall Street
   B. south on John Street, then west on 6th Avenue, then south on Eastern Boulevard, then east on 5th Avenue, then north on Hall Street

C. south on John Street, then west on 6th Avenue, then south on Clark Street, then east on 4th Avenue, then north on Eastern Boulevard, then east on 5th Avenue, then north on Hall Street
D. south on John Street, then west on 4th Avenue, then north on Hall Street

7. Traffic Enforcement Agent Murphy is on motorized patrol on 7th Avenue between Oak Street and Pearl Street when Lt. Robertson radios him to go to Jefferson High School, located on 5th Avenue between Lane Street and Oak Street. Which one of the following is the SHORTEST route for Agent Murphy to take, making sure to obey all the traffic regulations?
Travel east on 7th Avenue, then south on _____, then east on 5th Avenue to Jefferson High School.

A. Clark Street, then west on 4th Avenue, then north on Hall Street
B. Pearl Street, then west on 4th Avenue, then north on Lane Street
C. Lewis Street, then west on 6th Avenue, then south on Hall Street
D. Lewis Street, then west on 4th Avenue, then north on Oak Street

8. Traffic Enforcement Agent Vasquez was on 4th Avenue and Eastern Boulevard when a motorist asked him for directions to the 58th Police Precinct, which is located on Lewis Street between 5th and 6th Avenues.
Which one of the following is the SHORTEST route for Agent Vasquez to direct the motorist to take, making sure to obey all traffic regulations.
Travel north on Eastern Boulevard, then east on _____ on Lewis Street to the 58th Police Precinct.

A. 5th Avenue, then north
B. 7th Avenue, then south
C. 6th Avenue, then north on Pearl Street, then east on 7th Avenue, then south
D. 5th Avenue, then north on Clark Street, then east on 6th Avenue, then south

Questions 9-13.

DIRECTIONS: Questions 9 through 13 are to be answered SOLELY on the basis of the following map and the following information.

Toll collectors answer motorists' questions concerning directions by reading a map of the metropolitan area. Although many alternate routes leading to destinations exist on the following map, you are to choose the MOST direct route of those given.

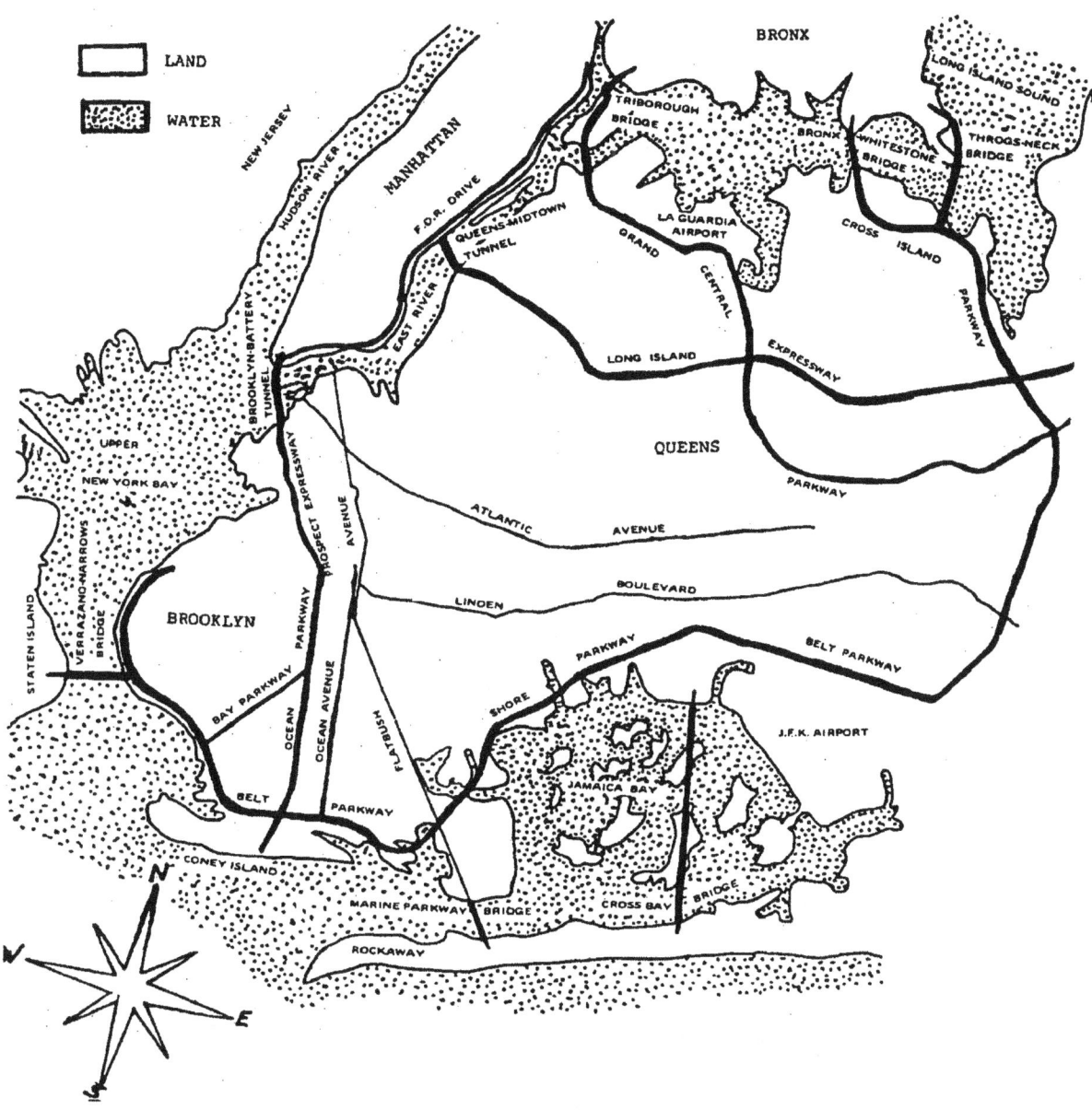

9. A motorist driving from the Bronx over the Triborough Bridge wants to go to LaGuardia Airport in Queens.
   The officer should direct him to

   A. Grand Central Parkway
   B. F.D.R. Drive
   C. Shore Parkway
   D. Flatbush Avenue

10. A motorist driving from Manhattan through the Queens Midtown Tunnel would travel DIRECTLY onto

    A. Shore Parkway
    B. F.D.R. Drive
    C. Long Island Expressway
    D. Atlantic Avenue

11. A motorist traveling north over the Marine Parkway Bridge should take which route to reach Coney Island?

    A. Shore Parkway East
    B. Belt Parkway West
    C. Linden Boulevard
    D. Ocean Parkway

12. Which facility does NOT connect the Bronx and Queens?

    A. Triborough Bridge
    B. Bronx-Whitestone Bridge
    C. Verrazano-Narrows Bridge
    D. Throgs-Neck Bridge

13. A motorist driving from Manhattan arrives at the toll booth of the Brooklyn-Battery Tunnel and asks directions to Ocean Parkway.
    To which one of the following routes should the motorist FIRST be directed?

    A. Atlantic Avenue
    B. Bay Parkway
    C. Prospect Expressway
    D. Ocean Avenue

Questions 14-16.

DIRECTIONS: Questions 14 through 16 are to be answered SOLELY on the basis of the following map. The flow of traffic is indicated by the arrows. If there is only one arrow shown, then traffic flows only in the direction indicated by the arrow. If there are two arrows, then traffic flows in both directions. You must follow the flow of traffic.

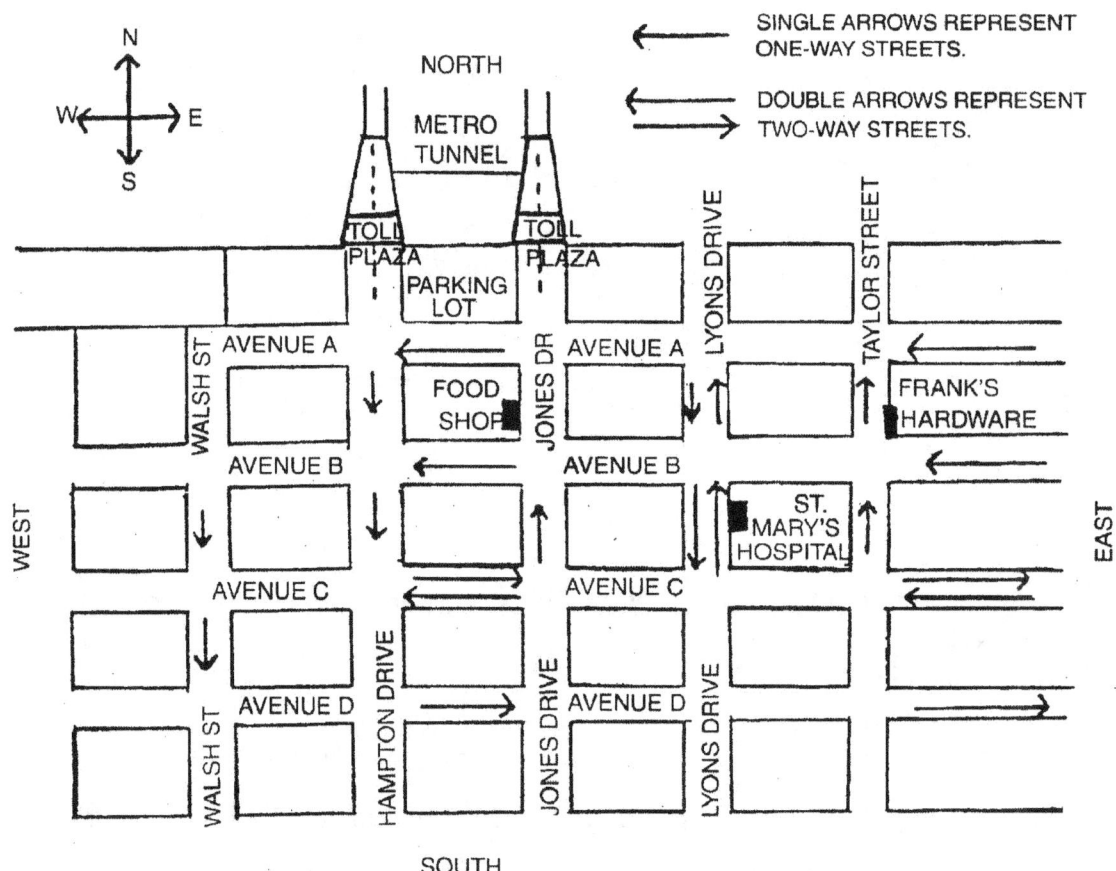

14. A motorist is exiting the Metro Tunnel and approaches the bridge and tunnel officer at the toll plaza. He asks the officer how to get to the food shop on Jones Drive. Which one of the following is the SHORTEST route for the motorist to take, making sure to obey all traffic regulations?
    Travel south on Hampton Drive, then left on _____ on Jones Drive to the food shop.

A.	Avenue A, then right	B.	Avenue B, then right
C.	Avenue D, then left	D.	Avenue C, then left

15. A motorist heading south pulls up to a toll booth at the exit of the Metro Tunnel and asks 15.____
Bridge and Tunnel Officer Evans how to get to Frank's Hardware Store on Taylor Street.
Which one of the following is the SHORTEST route for the motorist to take, making
sure to obey all traffic regulations?
Travel south on Hampton Drive, then east on

   A. Avenue B to Taylor Street
   B. Avenue D, then north on Taylor Street to Avenue B
   C. Avenue C, then north on Taylor Street to Avenue B
   D. Avenue C, then north on Lyons Drive, then east on Avenue B to Taylor Street

16. A motorist is exiting the Metro Tunnel and approaches the toll plaza. She asks Bridge 16.____
and Tunnel Officer Owens for directions to St. Mary's Hospital.
Which one of the following is the SHORTEST route for the motorist to take, making
sure to obey all traffic regulations?
Travel south on Hampton Drive, then _____ on Lyons Drive to St. Mary's Hospital.

   A. left on Avenue D, then left
   B. right on Avenue A, then left on Walsh Street, then left on Avenue D, then left
   C. left on Avenue C, then left
   D. left on Avenue B, then right

Questions 17-18.

DIRECTIONS: Questions 17 and 18 are to be answered SOLELY on the basis of the map which appears on the following page. The flow of traffic is indicated by the arrows. If there is only one arrow shown, then traffic flows only in the direction indicated by the arrow. If there are two arrows shown, then traffic flows in both directions. You must follow the flow of traffic.

8 (#1)

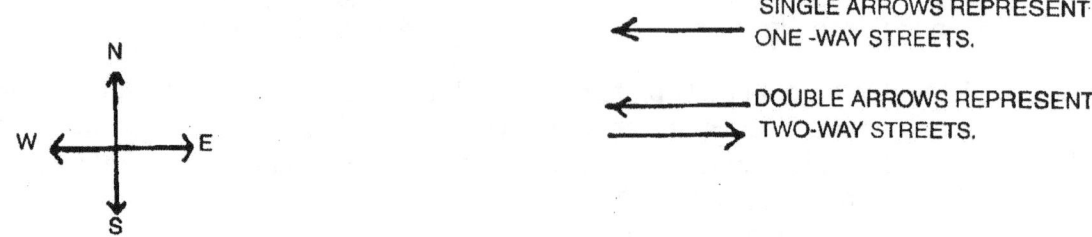

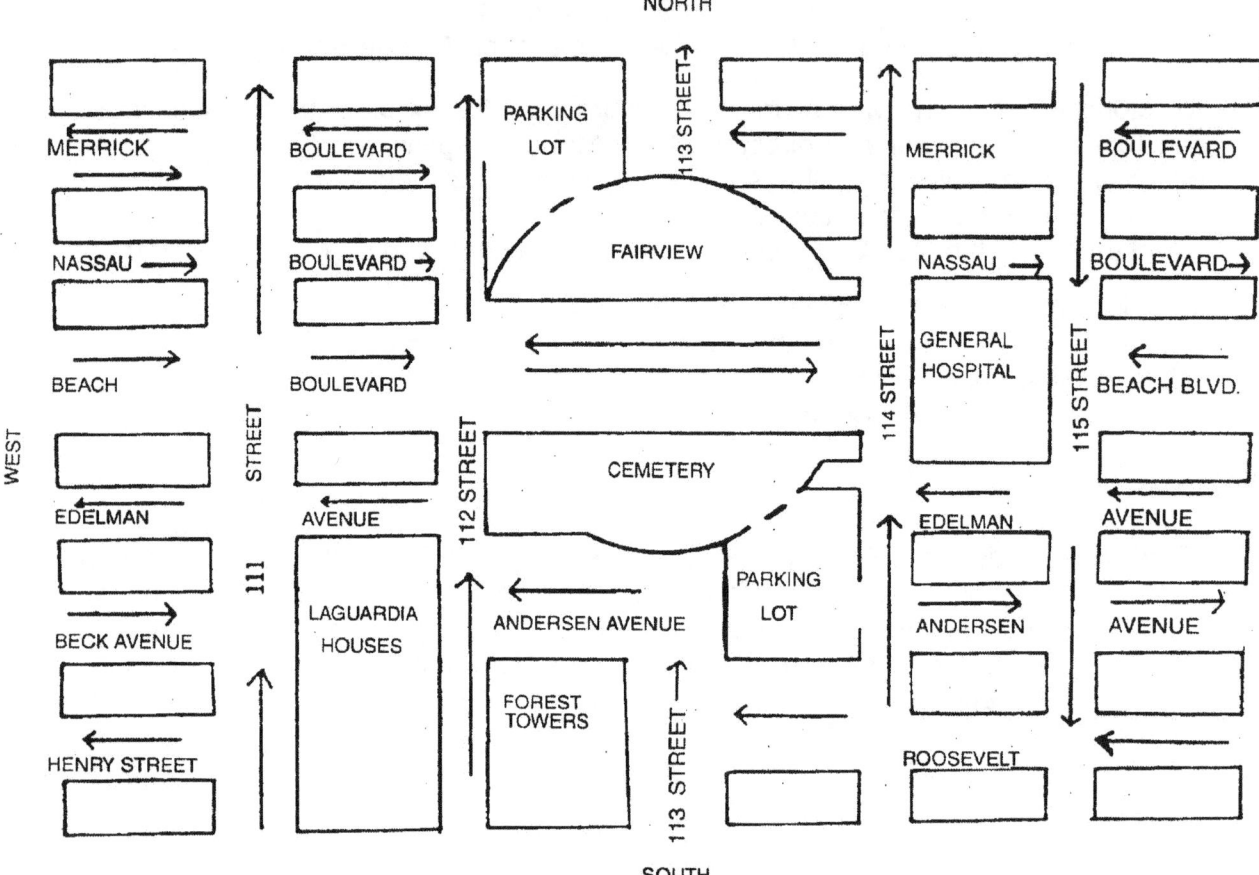

17. Police Officers Glenn and Albertson are on 111th Street at Henry Street when they are dispatched to a past robbery at Beach Boulevard and 115th Street.
Which one of the following is the SHORTEST route for the officers to follow in their patrol car, making sure to obey all traffic regulations?
Travel north on lllth Street, then east on _____ south on 115th Street.

17. ____

   A. Edelman Avenue, then north on 112th Street, then east on Beach Boulevard, then north on 114th Street, then east on Nassau Boulevard, then one block
   B. Beach Boulevard, then north on 114th Street, then east on Nassau Boulevard, then one block
   C. Merrick Boulevard, then two blocks
   D. Nassau Boulevard, then south on 112th Street, then east on Beach Boulevard, then north on 114th Street, then east on Nassau Boulevard, then one block

74

18. Later in their tour, Officers Glenn and Albertson are driving on 114th Street. If they make a left turn to enter the parking lot at Andersen Avenue, and then make a u-turn, in what direction would they now be headed?

    A. North   B. South   C. East   D. West

18.____

Questions 19-20.

DIRECTIONS: Questions 19 and 20 are to be answered SOLELY on the basis of the following map. The flow of traffic is indicated by the arrows. If there is only one arrow shown, then traffic flows only in the direction indicated by the arrow. If there are two arrows shown, then traffic flows in both directions. You must follow the flow of traffic.

19. You are located at Apple Avenue and White Street. You receive a call to respond to the corner of Lydig Avenue and Pilot Street.
Which one of the following is the MOST direct route for you to take in your patrol car, making sure to obey all traffic regulations?
Travel _____ on Pilot Street.

    A. two blocks south on White Street, then one block east on Canton Avenue, then one block north on Hudson Street, then three blocks west on Bear Avenue, then three blocks south
    B. one block south on White Street, then two blocks west on Bear Avenue, then three blocks south

19.____

C. two blocks west on Apple Avenue, then four blocks south
D. two blocks south on White Street, then one block west on Canton Avenue, then three blocks south on Mariner Street, then one block west on Vista Avenue, then one block north

20. You are located at Canton Avenue and Pilot Street. You receive a call of a crime in progress at the intersection of Canton Avenue and Hudson Street.
Which one of the following is the MOST direct route for you to take in your patrol car, making sure to obey all traffic regulations?
Travel

   A. two blocks north on Pilot Street, then two blocks east on Apple Avenue, then one block south on White Street, then one block east on Bear Avenue, then one block south on Hudson Street
   B. three blocks south on Pilot Street, then travel one block east on Vista Avenue, then travel three blocks north on Mariner Street, then travel two blocks east on Canton Avenue
   C. one block north on Pilot Street, then travel three blocks east on Bear Avenue, then travel one block south on Hudson Street
   D. two blocks north on Pilot Street, then travel three blocks east on Apple Avenue, then travel two blocks south on Hudson Street

20.____

KEY (CORRECT ANSWERS)

1.	B	11.	B/D
2.	D	12.	C
3.	B	13.	C
4.	C	14.	D
5.	A	15.	C
6.	D	16.	C
7.	A	17.	B
8.	B	18.	C
9.	A	19.	B
10.	C	20.	D

EVALUATING INFORMATION AND EVIDENCE
EXAMINATION SECTION
TEST 1

DIRECTIONS: Each question or incomplete statement is followed by several suggested answers or completions. Select the one that BEST answers the question or completes the statement. *PRINT THE LETTER OF THE CORRECT ANSWER IN THE SPACE AT THE RIGHT.*

Questions 1-9

Questions 1 through 9 measure your ability to (1) determine whether statements from witnesses say essentially the same thing and (2) determine the evidence needed to make it reasonably certain that a particular conclusion is true.

1. Which of the following pairs of statements say essentially the same thing in two different ways?
    I. All Hoxie steelworkers are at least six feet tall. No steelworker is less than six feet tall.
    II. Some neutered pit bulls are not dangerous dogs. Some dangerous dogs are neutered pit bulls.

    A. I only
    B. I and II
    C. II only
    D. Neither I nor II

1.____

2. Which of the following pairs of statements say essentially the same thing in two different ways?
    I. If we are in training today, it is definitely Wednesday. Every Wednesday there is training.
    II. You may go out tonight only after you clean your room. If you clean your room, you may go out tonight.

    A. I only
    B. I and II
    C. II only
    D. Neither I nor II

2.____

3. Which of the following pairs of statements say essentially the same thing in two different ways?
    I. The case will be dismissed if either the defendant pleads guilty and agrees to perform community service, or the defendant pleads guilty and makes a full apology to the victim.
    The case will be dismissed if the defendant pleads guilty and either agrees to perform community service or makes a full apology to the victim.
    II. Long books are fun to read.
    Books that aren't fun to read aren't long.

    A. I only
    B. I and II
    C. II only
    D. Neither I nor II

3.____

77

4. Which of the following pairs of statements say essentially the same thing in two different ways?
   I. If you live in a mansion, you have a big heating bill. If you do not have a big heating bill, you do not live in a mansion.
   II. Some clerks can both type and read shorthand. Some clerks can neither type nor read shorthand.

   A. I only
   B. I and II
   C. II only
   D. Neither I nor II

5. Summary of Evidence Collected to Date:
   I. Three students - Bob, Mary and Stan - each received a grade of A, C and F on the civil service exam.
   II. Stan did not receive an F on the exam.

   Prematurely Drawn Conclusion: Stan received an A.
   Which of the following pieces of evidence, if any, would make it *reasonably certain* that the conclusion drawn is true?

   A. Bob received an F
   B. Mary received a C
   C. Bob did not receive an A
   D. None of these

6. Summary of Evidence Collected to Date:
   I. At Walco, all the employees who work the morning shift work the evening shift as well.
   II. Some Walco employees who work the evening shift also work the afternoon shift.

   Prematurely Drawn Conclusion: If Ron, a Walco employee, works the morning shift, he does not work the afternoon shift.
   Which of the following pieces of evidence, if any, would make it *reasonably certain* that the conclusion drawn is true?

   A. Ron works only two shifts
   B. Ron works the evening shift
   C. All Walco employees work at least one shift
   D. None of these

7. Summary of Evidence Collected to Date:

   All the family counselors at the agency have an MTF certification and an advanced degree.

   Prematurely Drawn Conclusion: Any employee of the agency who has an advanced degree is a family counselor.

   Which of the following pieces of evidence, if any, would make it *reasonably certain* that the conclusion drawn is true?

A. Nobody at the agency who has an advanced degree is employed as anything other than a family counselor
B. Everyone who has an MTF certification is a family counselor
C. Each person at the agency who has an MTF certification also has an advanced degree
D. None of these

8. <u>Summary of Evidence Collected to Date:</u>
Margery, a worker at the elder agency, is working on recreational programs.
<u>Prematurely Drawn Conclusion:</u> Margery is not working on cases of elder abuse.
Which of the following pieces of evidence, if any, would make it *reasonably certain* that the conclusion drawn is true?

   A. Elder abuse and recreational programs are unrelated fields
   B. Nobody at the elder agency who works on cases of elder abuse works on recreation programs
   C. Nobody at the elder agency who works on recreational programs works on cases of elder abuse
   D. None of these

9. <u>Summary of Evidence Collected to Date:</u>
   I. St. Leo's Cathedral is not as tall as the FarCorp building.
   II. The FarCorp building and the Hyatt Uptown are the same height.
<u>Prematurely Drawn Conclusion:</u> The FarCorp building is not in Springfield.
Which of the following pieces of evidence, if any, would make it *reasonably certain* that the conclusion drawn is true?

   A. No buildings in Springfield are as tall as the Hyatt Uptown
   B. The Hyatt Uptown is not in Springfield
   C. St. Leo's Cathedral is the oldest building in Springfield
   D. None of these

Questions 10-14

Questions 10 through 14 refer to Map #1 and measure your ability to orient yourself within a given section of town, neighborhood or particular area. Each of the questions describes a starting point and a destination. Assume that you are driving a car in the area shown on the map accompanying the questions. Use the map as a basis for the shortest way to get from one point to another without breaking the law.

On the map, a street marked by arrows, or by arrows and the words "One Way," indicates one-way travel, and should be assumed to be one-way for the entire length, even when there are breaks or jogs in the street.

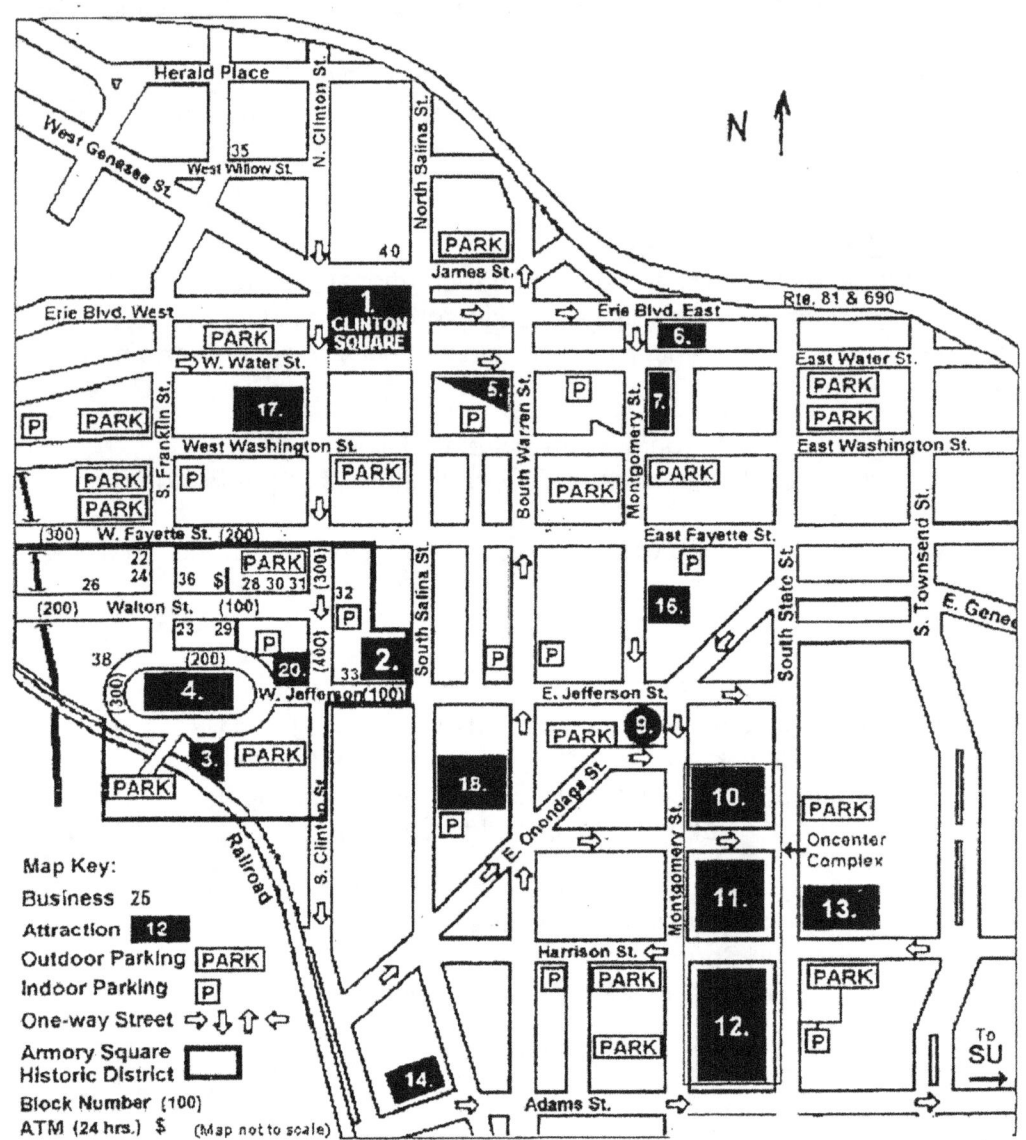

Map #1

1. Clinton Square
2. Landmark Theatre
3. OnTrack Commuter Rail Service
4. Museum of Science and Technology
5. Hanover Square
6. Erie Canal Museum
7. City Hall
9. Columbus Circle
10. Mulroy Civic Center Theaters
11. War Memorial
12. Convention Center
13. Everson Museum of Art
14. Convention and Visitors Bureau
16. Onondaga Historical Association
17. Federal Plaza
18. Galleries of Syracuse

10. The shortest legal way from Columbus Circle to Federal Plaza is 10._____

    A. west on Jefferson St., north on Salina St., west on Water St.
    B. east on Jefferson St., north on State St., west on Washington St.
    C. north on Montgomery St., west on Washington St.
    D. south on Montgomery St., west on Harrison St., north on Salina St., west on Washington St.

11. The shortest legal way from Clinton Square to the Museum of Science and Technology is 11._____

    A. south on Clinton St., west on Fayette St., south on Franklin St.
    B. west on Erie Blvd., south on Franklin St.
    C. south on Clinton St., west on Water St., south on Franklin St.
    D. south on Clinton St., west on Jefferson St.

12. The shortest legal way from Hanover Square to Landmark Theatre is 12._____

    A. west on Water St., south on Salina St.
    B. east on Water St., south on Montgomery St., west on Fayette St., south on Salina St.
    C. east on Water St., south on Montgomery St., west on Fayette St., south on Clinton St., east on Jefferson St.
    D. south on Warren St., west on Jefferson St.

13. The shortest legal way from the Convention Center to the Erie Canal Museum is 13._____

    A. north on State St., west on Washington St., north on Montgomery St.
    B. north on Montgomery St., jog west on Jefferson St., north on Montgomery St.
    C. north on State St., west on Fayette St., north on Warren St., east on Water St.
    D. north on State St., west on Water St.

14. The shortest legal way from City Hall to Clinton Square is 14._____

    A. west on Washington St., north on Salina St.
    B. south on Montgomery St., west on Fayette St., north on Salina St.
    C. north on Montgomery St., west on Erie Blvd.
    D. west on Water St.

Questions 15-19

Questions 15 through 19 refer to Figure #1, on the following page, and measure your ability to understand written descriptions of events. Each question presents a description of an accident or event and asks you which of the five drawings in Figure #1 BEST represents it.

In the drawings, the following symbols are used:

Moving vehicle: ⌂   Non-moving vehicle: ⬆

Pedestrian or bicycle: ●

The path and direction of travel of a vehicle or pedestrian is indicated by a solid line.

The path and direction of travel of each vehicle or pedestrian directly involved in a collision from the point of impact is indicated by a dotted line.

In the space at the right, print the letter of the drawing that best fits the descriptions written below:

15. A driver heading north on Elm sideswipes a parked car, veers into the oncoming lane and travels through the intersection of Elm and Main. He then sideswipes an oncoming car, veers back into the northbound lane and flees. 15._____

16. A driver heading south on Elm sideswipes a car parked in the southbound lane, then loses control and veers through the intersection of Elm and Main. The driver then collides with the rear of another parked car, which is knocked forward after the impact. 16._____

17. A driver heading north on Elm strikes the rear of a parked car, which is knocked through the intersection of Elm and Main and strikes a parked car in the southbound lane head-on. 17._____

18. A driver heading north on Elm strikes the rear of a car that is stopped at a traffic light. The car at the light is knocked through the intersection of Elm and Main and strikes a parked car in the rear. 18._____

19. A driver heading south on Elm loses control and crosses into the other lane of traffic, where he sideswipes a car parked in the northbound lane, then veers back into the southbound lane, travels through the intersection of Elm and Main and collides with the rear end of a parked car. 19._____

FIGURE #1

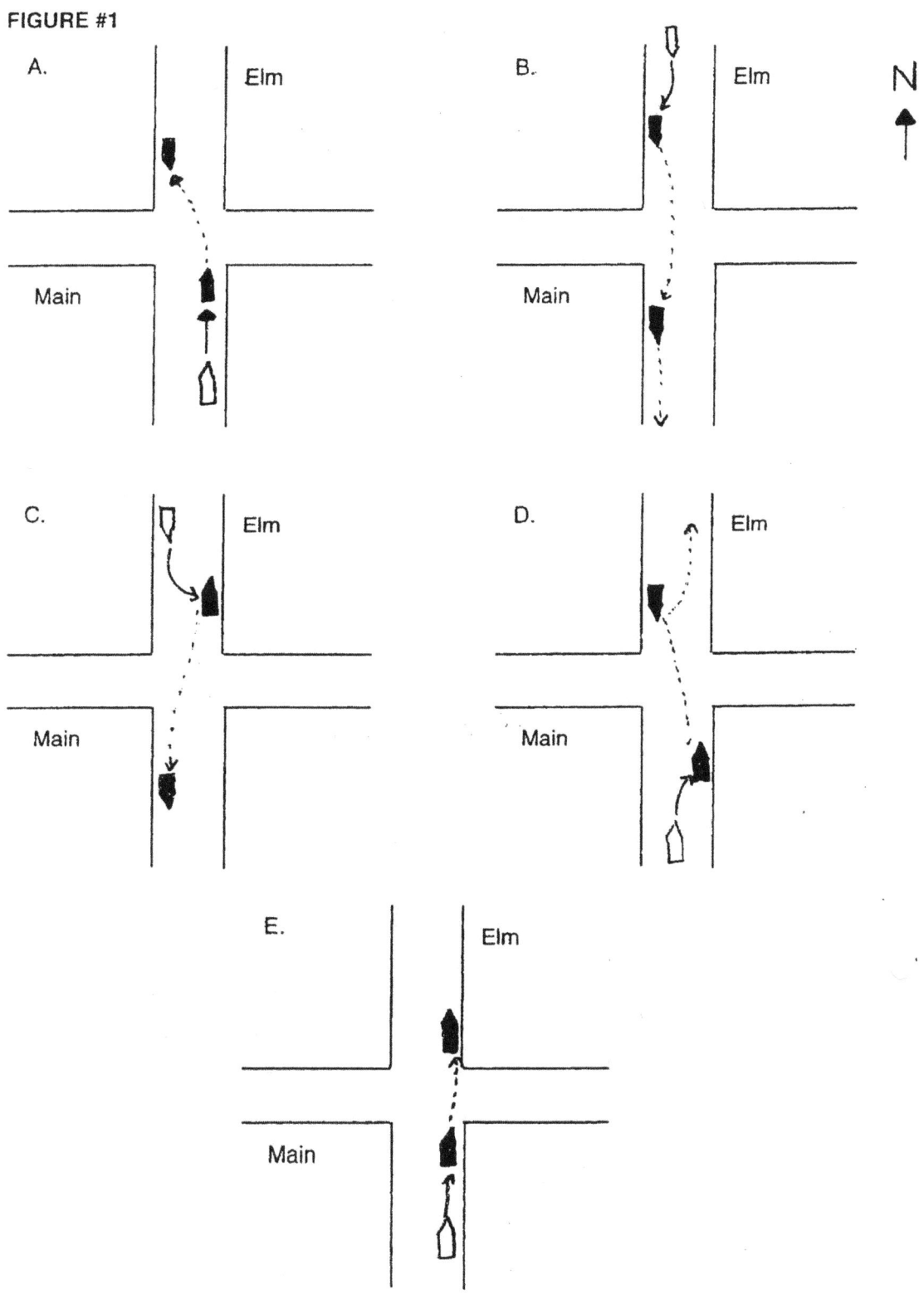

Questions 20-22

In questions 20 through 22, choose the word or phrase CLOSEST in meaning to the word or phrase printed in capital letters.

20. REDRESS

    A. suspend
    B. repeat
    C. compensate
    D. subdue

21. PRECEDENT

    A. cohort
    B. example
    C. obstruction
    D. elder

22. ADJUDICATION

    A. case
    B. judgment
    C. claim
    D. defendant

Questions 23-25

Questions 23 through 25 measure your ability to do fieldwork-related arithmetic. Each question presents a separate arithmetic problem for you to solve.

23. The Department of Sanitation purchased seven vehicles in the last year. Four of the vehicles were street sweepers that cost $95,000 each. Three were garbage compactors that cost $160,000 each. The average price of a vehicle purchased by the Department in the last year was about

    A. $98,000
    B. $108,000
    C. $122,000
    D. $145,000

24. Agent Frederick, whose car gets about 24 miles to the gallon, drives to Buffalo, 260 miles away. The average price of gasoline is $2.30 a gallon. How much did Agent Frederick spend on gas for the trip to Buffalo?

    A. $11   B. $25   C. $55   D. $113

25. Over the last four days, Precinct 11 has had 20 misdemeanor arrests each day. If the precinct records 15 misdemeanor arrests on the fifth day, what will its average daily number of misdemeanor arrests be?

    A. 16   B. 17   C. 18   D. 19

KEY (CORRECT ANSWERS)

1.	D	11.	A
2.	C	12.	B
3.	A	13.	C
4.	A	14.	A
5.	B	15.	D
6.	A	16.	B
7.	A	17.	A
8.	C	18.	E
9.	A	19.	C
10.	B	20.	C

21. B
22. B
23. C
24. B
25. D

TEST 2

DIRECTIONS: Each question or incomplete statement is followed by several suggested answers or completions. Select the one that BEST answers the question or completes the statement. *PRINT THE LETTER OF THE CORRECT ANSWER IN THE SPACE AT THE RIGHT.*

Questions 1-9

Questions 1 through 9 measure your ability to (1) determine whether statements from witnesses say essentially the same thing and (2) determine the evidence needed to make it reasonably certain that a particular conclusion is true.
To do well on this part of the test, you do NOT have to have a working knowledge of police procedures and techniques. Nor do you have to have any more familiarity with criminals and criminal behavior than that acquired from reading newspapers, listening to radio or watching TV. To do well in this part, you must read and reason carefully.

1. Which of the following pairs of statements say essentially the same thing in two different ways?
    I. All of the teachers at the school are wise, but some have proven to be bad-tempered.
       Teachers at the school are either wise or bad-tempered.
    II. If John can both type and do long division, he is qualified for this job.
        If John applies for this job, he can both type and do long division.

    A. I only
    B. I and II
    C. II only
    D. Neither I nor II

2. Which of the following pairs of statements say essentially the same thing in two different ways?
    I. If Carl rides the A train, the C train is down.
       Carl doesn't ride the A train unless the C train is down.
    II. If the three sides of a triangle are equal, the triangle is equilateral.
        A triangle is equilateral if the three sides are equal.

    A. I only
    B. I and II
    C. II only
    D. Neither I nor II

3. Which of the following pairs of statements say essentially the same thing in two different ways?
    I. If this dog has a red collar, it must be Slim.
       If this dog does not have a red collar, it can't be Slim.
    II. Dr. Slouka is not in his office during lunchtime.
        If it's not lunchtime, Dr. Slouka is in his office.

    A. I only
    B. I and II
    C. II only
    D. Neither I nor II

4. Which of the following pairs of statements say essentially the same thing in two different ways?
   I. At least one caseworker at Social Services has a degree in psychology.
      Not all the caseworkers at Social Services have a degree in psychology.
   II. If an officer doesn't pass the physical fitness test, he cannot be promoted.
       If an officer is not promoted, he hasn't passed the physical fitness test.

   A. I only
   B. I and II
   C. II only
   D. Neither I nor II

5. Summary of Evidence Collected to Date:
   I. All the Class II inspectors use multiplication when they inspect escalators.
   II. On some days, Fred, a Class II inspector, doesn't use multiplication at all.
   III. Fred's friend, Garth, uses multiplication every day.
   Prematurely Drawn Conclusion: Garth inspects escalators every day.
   Which of the following pieces of evidence, if any, would make it *reasonably certain* that the conclusion drawn is true?

   A. Garth is a Class II inspector
   B. Fred never inspects escalators
   C. Fred usually doesn't inspect escalators
   D. None of these

6. Summary of Evidence Collected to Date:
   I. Every one of the shelter's male pit bulls has been neutered.
   II. Some male pit bulls have also been muzzled.
   Prematurely Drawn Conclusion: Rex has been neutered.
   Which of the following pieces of evidence, if any, would make it *reasonably certain* that the conclusion drawn is true?

   A. Rex, a pit bull at the shelter, has been muzzled
   B. All of the pit bulls at the shelter are males
   C. Rex is one of the shelter's male pit bulls
   D. None of these

7. Summary of Evidence Collected to Date:
   I. Some of the social workers at the clinic have been welfare recipients.
   II. Some of the social workers at the clinic are college graduates.
   Prematurely Drawn Conclusion: Some of the social workers at the clinic who are college graduates have never received welfare benefits.
   Which of the following pieces of evidence, if any, would make it *reasonably certain* that the conclusion drawn is true?

   A. There are more college graduates at the clinic than those who have received welfare benefits
   B. There is an odd number of social workers at the clinic
   C. The number of college graduates and former welfare recipients at the clinic is the same
   D. None of these

8. Summary of Evidence Collected to Date:
   Everyone who works at the library has read *War and Peace*. Most people who have read *War and Peace* have also read *Anna Karenina*.
   Prematurely Drawn Conclusion: Marco has read *War and Peace*.
   Which of the following pieces of evidence, if any, would make it *reasonably certain* that the conclusion drawn is true?

   A. Marco works at the library
   B. Marco has probably read *Anna Karenina*
   C. Everyone who has read *Anna Karenina* has read *War and Peace*
   D. None of these

9. Summary of Evidence Collected to Date:
   Officer Skiles is working on the Martin investigation.
   Prematurely Drawn Conclusion: Skiles is also working on the Bartlett case.
   Which of the following pieces of evidence, if any, would make it *reasonably certain* that the conclusion drawn is true?

   A. Everyone who is working on the Martin investigation is also working on the Bartlett investigation
   B. Everyone who is working on the Bartlett investigation is also working on the Martin investigation
   C. The Martin investigation and Bartlett investigation are being conducted at the same time
   D. None of these

Questions 10-14

Questions 10 through 14 refer to Map #2 and measure your ability to orient yourself within a given section of town, neighborhood or particular area. Each of the questions describes a starting point and a destination. Assume that you are driving a car in the area shown on the map accompanying the questions. Use the map as a basis for the shortest way to get from one point to another without breaking the law.

On the map, a street marked by arrows, or by arrows and the words "One Way," indicates one-way travel, and should be assumed to be one-way for the entire length, even when there are breaks or jogs in the street. EXCEPTION: A street that does not have the same name over the full length.

4 (#2)

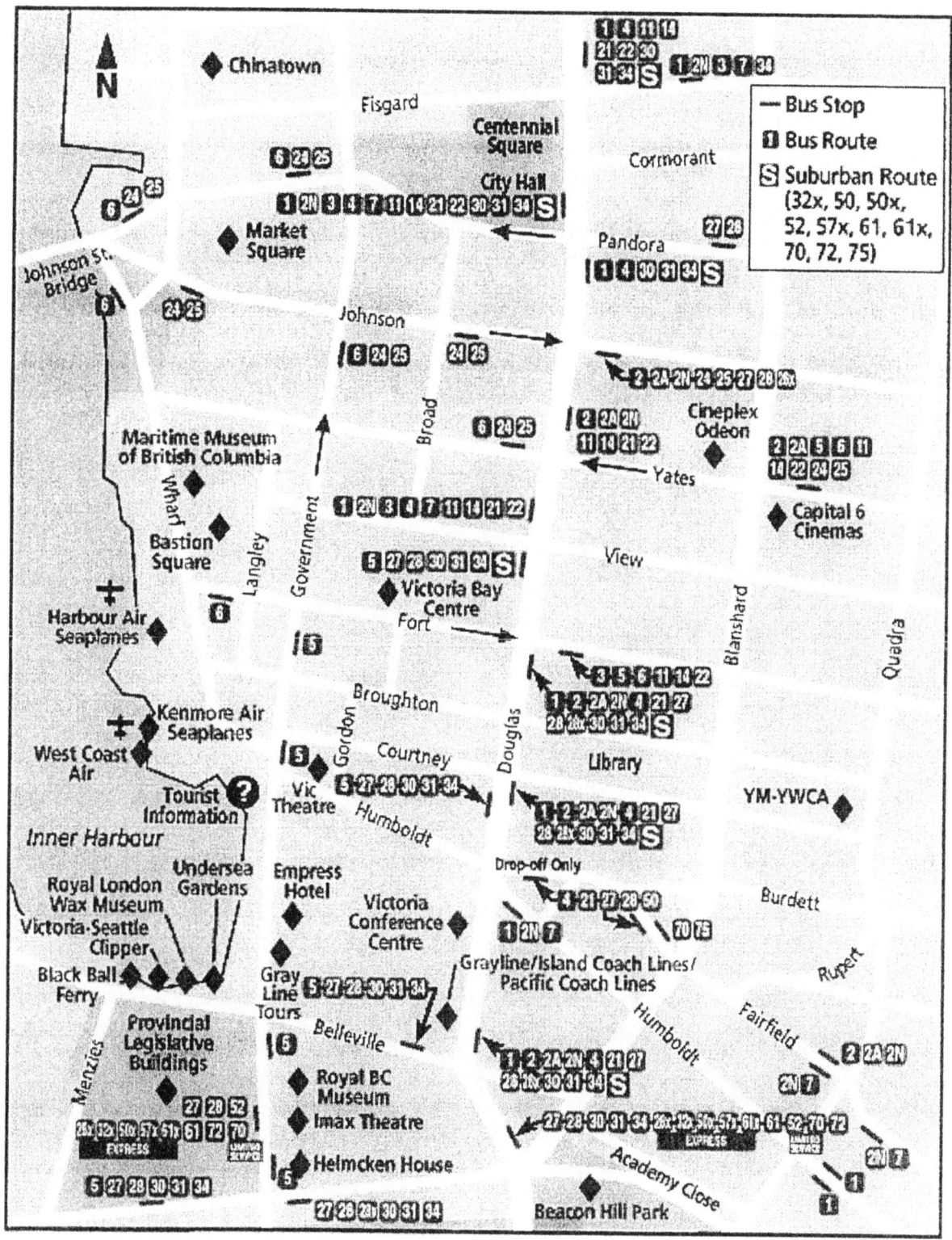

Map #2

10. The shortest legal way from the Royal London Wax Museum to the Chinatown block is 10._____

    A. east on Belleville, north on Douglas, west on Broughton, north on Government
    B. east on Belleville, north on Government
    C. east on Belleville, north on Government, west on Yates, north on Wharf
    D. east on Belleville, north on Douglas, west on Fisgard

11. The shortest legal way from the Maritime Museum of British Columbia to the Victoria Conference Centre is 11._____

    A. north on Wharf, east on Yates, south on Douglas
    B. south and west on Wharf, north on Government, east on Broughton, south on Douglas
    C. south on Wharf, east on Fort, south on Douglas
    D. south and west on Wharf, south on Government, east on Belleville, north on Douglas

12. The shortest legal way from Market Square to City Hall is 12._____

    A. north on Government, east on Fisgard, south on Douglas
    B. east on Pandora, north on Douglas
    C. east on Johnson, north on Blanshard, west on Pandora, north on Douglas
    D. east on Johnson, north on Douglas

13. The shortest legal way from the Victoria Bay Centre to Bastion Square is 13._____

    A. east on Fort, south on Douglas, west on Broughton, north on Wharf
    B. west on Fort, north on Government, west on Yates, south on Wharf
    C. west on Fort, north on Wharf
    D. east on Fort, north on Douglas, west on Johnson, south on Wharf

14. The shortest legal way from The Empress Hotel to the YM-YWCA is 14._____

    A. north on Government, east on Broughton
    B. north on Government, east on Courtney
    C. north on Government, southeast on Humboldt, north on Quadra
    D. north on Government, west on Courtney

Questions 15-19

Questions 15 through 19 refer to Figure #2, on the following page, and measure your ability to understand written descriptions of events. Each question presents a description of an accident or event and asks you which of the five drawings in Figure #2 BEST represents it.

In the drawings, the following symbols are used:

Moving vehicle: ◊   Non-moving vehicle: ◆

Pedestrian or bicycle: ●

The path and direction of travel of a vehicle or pedestrian is indicated by a solid line.

The path and direction of travel of each vehicle or pedestrian directly involved in a collision from the point of impact is indicated by a dotted line.

In the space at the right, print the letter of the drawing that best fits the descriptions written below:

15. A driver traveling north on Taylor strikes a parked car in the rear and knocks it forward, where it collides with a pedestrian in the crosswalk. 15.____

16. A driver headed south on Taylor strikes another car that is traveling east through the intersection of Taylor and Hayes. After the impact, the eastbound car veers to the right and strikes a pedestrian in the crosswalk on Jones. 16.____

17. A driver headed south on Taylor runs a red light and strikes another car that is headed east on Hayes. The eastbound car is knocked into a pedestrian that is using the crosswalk on Taylor 17.____

18. A driver traveling south on Taylor makes a sudden left turn onto Hayes. In the intersection, he strikes the front of an oncoming car and veers onto Hayes, where he strikes a pedestrian in the crosswalk. 18.____

19. A driver headed west on Hayes strikes a car that is traveling east through the intersection of Taylor and Hayes. After the impact, the eastbound car veers to the right and strikes a pedestrian in the crosswalk on Jones. 19.____

FIGURE #2

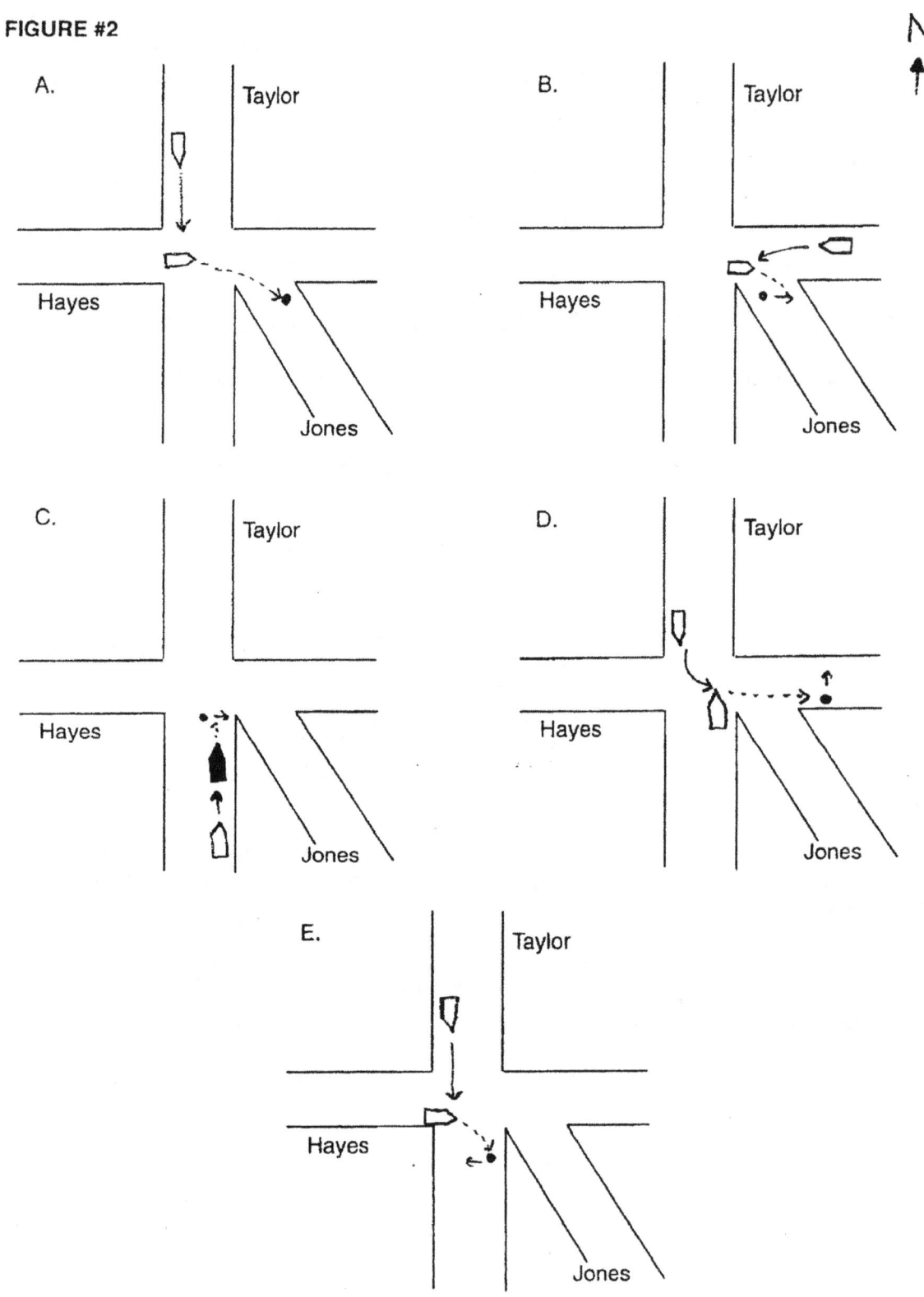

Questions 20-22

In questions 20 through 22, choose the word or phrase CLOSEST in meaning to the word or phrase printed in capital letters.

20. SEQUESTER

    A. follow
    B. separate
    C. endorse
    D. punish

21. EXECUTE

    A. carry out
    B. advance
    C. impede
    D. occur

22. SUPPRESS

    A. uphold
    B. convict
    C. forbid
    D. compensate

Questions 23-25

Questions 23 through 25 measure your ability to do fieldwork-related arithmetic. Each question presents a separate arithmetic problem for you to solve..

23. In the election for the presidency of Local Union 1134, Stan Fitz received 542 votes, Elizabeth Stuckey received 430 votes and Gene Sterner received 130 votes. Ninety percent of those eligible to vote did so. What was the number of eligible voters?

    A. 900
    B. 992
    C. 1102
    D. 1224

24. The Department of Records wants to sort its files alphabetically into boxes that hold an average of 50 files each. The Department has 1,140 records, an amount that is expected to double in the next ten years. To have enough boxes ten years from now, the Department should buy at least _____ boxes.

    A. 23   B. 38   C. 45   D. 47

25. The office's petty cash fund contains a total of $433 on Wednesday. At the beginning of the day, Arnold reimburses $270 that he had previously borrowed from the fund. Then Janet withdraws $158 for office supplies; Hank spends $87 on lunch for a committee meeting; and at the end of the day, Ernestine buys a new office calendar for $12. How much remains in the petty cash fund at the end of the day on Wednesday?

    A. $94   B. $257   C. $446   D. $527

KEY (CORRECT ANSWERS)

1. D
2. B
3. A
4. D
5. A

6. C
7. D
8. A
9. A
10. B

11. C
12. D
13. A
14. B
15. C

16. A
17. E
18. D
19. B
20. B

21. A
22. C
23. D
24. D
25. C

READING COMPREHENSION
UNDERSTANDING AND INTERPRETING WRITTEN MATERIAL

EXAMINATION SECTION

TEST 1

DIRECTIONS: Each question or incomplete statement is followed by several suggested answers or completions. Select the one that BEST answers the question or completes the statement. *PRINT THE LETTER OF THE CORRECT ANSWER IN THE SPACE AT THE RIGHT.*

Questions 1-6.

DIRECTIONS: Questions 1 through 6 are to be answered SOLELY on the basis of the information contained in the following passage.

Duplicating is the process of making a number of identical copies of letters, documents, etc. from an original. Some duplicating processes make copies directly from the original document. Other duplicating processes require the preparation of a special master, and copies are then made from the master. Four of the most common duplicating processes are stencil, fluid, offset, and xerox.

In the stencil process, the typewriter is used to cut the words into a master called a stencil. Drawings, charts, or graphs can be cut into the stencil using a stylus. As many as 3,500 good-quality copies can be reproduced from one stencil. Various grades of finished paper from inexpensive mimeograph to expensive bond can be used.

The fluid process is a good method of copying from 50 to 125 good-quality copies from a master, which is prepared with a special dye. The master is placed on the duplicator, and special paper with a hard finish is moistened and then passed through the duplicator. Some of the dye on the master is dissolved, creating an impression on the paper. The impression becomes lighter as more copies are made; and once the dye on the master is used up, a new master must be made.

The offset process is the most adaptable office duplicating process because this process can be used for making a few copies or many copies. Masters can be made on paper or plastic for a few hundred copies, or on metal plates for as many as 75,000 copies. By using a special technique called photo-offset, charts, photographs, illustrations, or graphs can be reproduced on the master plate. The offset process is capable of producing large quantities of fine, top-quality copies on all types of finished paper.

The xerox process reproduces an exact duplicate from an original. It is the fastest duplicating method because the original material is placed directly on the duplicator, eliminating the need to make a special master. Any kind of paper can be used. The xerox process is the most expensive duplicating process; however, it is the best method of reproducing small quantities of good-quality copies of reports, letters, official documents, memos, or contracts.

1. Of the following, the MOST efficient method of reproducing 5,000 copies of a graph is
   A. stencil   B. fluid   C. offset   D. Xerox

2. The offset process is the MOST adaptable office duplicating process because
   A. it is the quickest duplicating method
   B. it is the least expensive duplicating method
   C. it can produce a small number or large number of copies
   D. a softer master can be used over and over again

3. Which one of the following duplicating processes uses moistened paper?
   A. Stencil   B. Fluid   C. Offset   D. Xerox

4. The fluid process would be the BEST process to use for reproducing
   A. five copies of a school transcript
   B. fifty copies of a memo
   C. five hundred copies of a form letter
   D. five thousand copies of a chart

5. Which one of the following duplicating processes does NOT require a special master?
   A. Fluid   B. Xerox   C. Offset   D. Stencil

6. Xerox is NOT used for all duplicating jobs because
   A. it produces poor-quality copies
   B. the process is too expensive
   C. preparing the master is too time-consuming

Questions 7-10.

DIRECTIONS: Questions 7 through 10 are to be answered SOLELY on the basis of the information contained in the following passage.

City government is committed to providing a safe and healthy work environment for all city employees. An effective agency safety program reduces accidents by educating employees about the types of careless acts which can cause accidents. Even in an office, accidents can happen. If each employee is aware of possible safety hazards, the number of accidents on the job can be reduced.

Careless use of office equipment can cause accidents and injuries. For example, file cabinet drawers which are filled with papers can be so heavy that the entire cabinet could tip over from the weight of one open drawer.

The bottom drawers of desks and file cabinets should never be left open since employees could easily trip over open drawers and injure themselves.

When reaching for objects on a high shelf, an employee should use a strong, sturdy object such as a step stool to stand on. Makeshift platforms made out of books, papers, or boxes can easily collapse. Even chairs can slide out from under foot, causing serious injury.

Even at an employee's desk, safety hazards can occur. Frayed or cut wires should be repaired or replaced immediately. Typewriters which are not firmly anchored to the desk or table could fall, causing injury.

Smoking is one of the major causes of fires in the office. A lighted match or improperly extinguished cigarette thrown into a wastebasket filled with paper could cause a major fire with possible loss of life. Where smoking is permitted, ashtrays should be used. Smoking is particularly dangerous in offices where flammable chemicals are used.

7. The goal of an effective safety program is to 7._____
    A. reduce office accidents
    B. stop employees from smoking on the job
    C. encourage employees to continue their education
    D. eliminate high shelves in offices

8. Desks and file cabinets can become safety hazards when 8._____
    A. their drawers are left open
    B. they are used as wastebaskets
    C. they are makeshift
    D. they are not anchored securely to the floor

9. Smoking is especially hazardous when it occurs 9._____
    A. near exposed wires
    B. in a crowded office
    C. in an area where flammable chemicals are used
    D. where books and papers are stored

10. Accidents are likely to occur when 10._____
    A. employees' desks are cluttered with books and papers
    B. employees are not aware of safety hazards
    C. employees close desk drawers
    D. step stools are used to reach high objects

Questions 11-18.

DIRECTIONS: Questions 11 through 18 are to be answered SOLELY on the basis of the information contained in the following passage.

The telephone directory is made up of two books. The first book consists of the introductory section and the alphabetical listing of names section. The second book is the classified directly (also known as the yellow pages). Many people who are familiar with one book do not realize how useful the other can be. The efficient office worker should become familiar with both books in order to make the best use of this important source of information.

The introductory section gives general instructions for finding numbers in the alphabetical listing and classified directory. This section also explains how to use the telephone company's many services, including the operator and information services, gives examples of charges for local and long distance calls, and lists area codes for the entire country. In addition, this section provides a useful postal zip code map.

The alphabetical listing of names section lists the names, addresses, and telephone numbers of subscribers in an area. Guide names, or *telltales*, are on the top corner of each page. These guide names indicate the first and last name to be found on that page. *Telltales* help locate any particular name quickly. A cross-reference spelling is also given to help locate names which are spelled several different ways. City, state, and federal government agencies are listed under the major government heading. For example, an agency of the federal government would be listed under *United States Government*.

The classified directory, or yellow pages, is a separate book. In this section are advertising services, public transportation line maps, shopping guides, and listing of businesses arranged by the type of product or services they offer. This book is most useful when looking for the name or phone number of a business when all that is known is the type of product offered and the address, or when trying to locate a particular type of business in an area. Businesses listed in the classified directory can usually be found in the alphabetical listing of names section. When the name of the business is known, you will find the address or phone number more quickly in the alphabetical listing of names section.

11. The introductory section provides
   A. shopping guides
   B. government listings
   C. business listings
   D. information services

12. Advertising services would be found in the
   A. introductory section
   B. alphabetical listing of names section
   C. classified directory
   D. information services

13. According to the information in the above passage for locating government agencies, the Information Office of the Department of Consumer Affairs of New York city government would be alphabetically listed FIRST under
   A. *I* for Information Offices
   B. *D* for Department of Consumer Affairs
   C. *N* for New York City
   D. *G* for government

14. When the name of a business is known, the QUICKEST way to find the phone number is to look in the
   A. classified directory
   B. introductory section
   C. alphabetical listing of names section
   D. advertising service section

15. The QUICKEST way to find the phone number of a business when the type of service a business offers and its address is known is to look in the
   A. classified directory
   B. alphabetical listing of names section
   C. introductory section
   D. information service

16. What is a *telltale*?
    A(n)
    A. alphabetical listing
    B. guide name
    C. map
    D. cross-reference listing

17. The BEST way to find a postal zip code is to look in the
    A. classified directory
    B. introductory section
    C. alphabetical listing of names section
    D. government heading

18. To help find names which have several different spellings, the telephone directory provides
    A. cross-reference spelling
    B. *telltales*
    C. spelling guides
    D. advertising services

Questions 19-24.

DIRECTIONS: Questions 19 through 24 are to be answered SOLELY on the basis of the information contained in the following instructions on sweeping.

SWEEPING

All sweeping must be done with damp sawdust, which is used to prevent the raising of dust when sweeping platforms and mezzanines. Soak sawdust thoroughly in a bucket of water for two to three hours before use. Drain before use so that no stains are left on concrete from excess water. In order to keep sawdust moist while being used, spread for an area of 120 feet in advance of actual sweeping. Never sweep sawdust over drains. To assure good footing, do not spread it on stairways or on damp or wet floor areas.

19. Dampened sawdust should be used when
    A. scrapping   B. dusting   C. sweeping   D. mopping

20. Of the following procedures, which is the CORRECT order to be followed when sweeping with sawdust?
    A. Soak, drain, and spread
    B. Spread, drain, and soak
    C. Spread, soak, and drain
    D. Drain, spread, and soak

21. Of the following, it is MOST correct to soak the sawdust in a bucket of water for _____ hour(s).
    A. a half-hour to an
    B. one to two
    C. two to three
    D. three to four

22. The water should be drained from the bucket of sawdust so that excess water does NOT
    A. cause passengers to lose their footing
    B. stain the concrete
    C. flood the tracks
    D. slow down the sweeping

23. Sawdust is dampened in order to
    A. assure good footing on stairways
    B. prevent the raising of dust when sweeping
    C. prevent the staining of concrete
    D. cool off platforms

24. The dampened sawdust may be spread on
    A. wet floors   B. drains   C. stairways   D. mezzanines

Questions 25-27.

DIRECTIONS: Questions 25 through 27 are to be answered SOLELY on the basis of the information contained in the following passage.

Whether a main lobby or upper corridor requires scrubbing or mopping and whether it should be done nightly or less frequently depends on the nature of the floor surface and the amount of traffic. In a building with heavy traffic, it may be desirable every night to scrub the main lobby and to mop the upper floor corridors. In such cases, it may also be found desirable to scrub the upper floors once a week. If traffic is light, it may be only necessary to mop the main lobby every other night and to mop the upper floor corridors once a week. If there is any traffic or usage at all, it will be necessary to at least sweep the corridors nightly.

25. According to the above passage, in a building with light traffic, the upper floor corridors should be
    A. swept every other night
    B. mopped every night
    C. swept nightly
    D. mopped every other night

26. According to the above passage, the number of times a floor is cleaned depends
    A. mainly on the type of floor surface
    B. mainly on the type of traffic
    C. only on the amount of traffic
    D. on both the floor surface and amount of traffic

27. According to the above passage, it may be DESIRABLE to have a heavily used main lobby swept
    A. daily and scrubbed weekly
    B. daily and mopped weekly
    C. and mopped weekly
    D. and scrubbed daily

Questions 28-30.

DIRECTIONS: Questions 28 through 30 are to be answered SOLELY on the basis of the information contained in the following passage.

SENIOR CITIZEN AND HANDICAPPED PASSSENGER REDUCED FARE PROGRAM

Upon display of his or her Medicare Card, Senior Citizen Reduced Fare Card, or Handicapped Photo I.D. Card to the Railroad Clerk on duty, and upon purchase of a token or evidence of having a token, a passenger will be issued a free return trip ticket. The passenger will then be directed to deposit full fare in a turnstile and enter the controlled area. Return trip tickets are valid 24 hours a day, 7 days a week, for the day of purchase and the following two (2) calendar days.

Each return trip ticket will be stamped with the station name and the date only at the time of issuing to a properly identified senior citizen or handicapped passenger. Overstamping of tickets is not allowed. Return trip tickets issued from 2300 hours will be stamped with the date of the following day.

On the return trip, the Railroad Clerk on duty will direct the passenger to enter the controlled area via the exit gate upon the passenger turning in the return trip ticket and displaying his/her Medicare Card, Senior Citizen Reduced Fare Card, or Handicapped Photo I.D. Card.

28. A Railroad Clerk issued a free return ticket to a senior citizen who displayed a birth certificate and a token. The Railroad Clerk's action was
    A. *proper*, because the Railroad Clerk had proof of the senior citizen's age
    B. *improper*, because the senior citizen did not display a Medicare Card, Senior Citizen Reduced Fair Card, or Handicapped Photo I.D. Card
    C. *proper*, because it is inconvenient for many senior citizens to obtain a Medicare Card, Senior Citizen Reduced Fare Card, or Handicapped Photo I.D. Card
    D. *improper*, because the senior citizen did not buy a token from the Railroad Clerk

28.____

29. The return trip ticket issued to a senior citizen is valid for ONLY
    A. 24 hours
    B. the day of purchase
    C. two days
    D. the day of purchase and the following two calendar days

29.____

30. A Railroad Clerk denied entry to the controlled area via the exit gate to an 18 year-old handicapped passenger who turned in a correctly stamped return trip ticket, but did not display any type of identification card.
The Railroad Clerk's action was
    A. *proper*, because the passenger should have displayed his Handicapped Photo I.D. Card
    B. *improper*, because the passenger turned in a correctly stamped return trip ticket
    C. *proper*, because the passenger should have displayed either his Handicapped Photo I.D. Card or Social Security Card
    D. *improper*, because it should have been obvious to the Railroad Clerk that the passenger was handicapped

30.____

KEY (CORRECT ANSWERS)

1.	C	11.	D	21.	C
2.	C	12.	C	22.	B
3.	B	13.	C	23.	B
4.	B	14.	C	24.	D
5.	B	15.	A	25.	C
6.	A	16.	B	26.	D
7.	A	17.	B	27.	D
8.	A	18.	A	28.	B
9.	C	19.	C	29.	D
10.	B	20.	A	30.	A

TEST 2

DIRECTIONS: Each question or incomplete statement is followed by several suggested answers or completions. Select the one that BEST answers the question or completes the statement. *PRINT THE LETTER OF THE CORRECT ANSWER IN THE SPACE AT THE RIGHT.*

Questions 1-2.

DIRECTIONS: Questions 1 and 2 are to be answered SOLELY on the basis of the information contained in the following passage.

The Commissioner of Investigation shall have general responsibility for the investigation and elimination of corrupt or other criminal activity, conflicts of interest, unethical conduct, misconduct, and incompetence by city agencies, by city officers and employees, and by persons regulated by, doing business with, or receiving funds directly or indirectly from the city, with respect to their dealings with the city. All agency heads shall be responsible for establishing, subject to review for completeness and inter-agency consistency by the Commissioner of Investigation, written standards of conduct for the officials and employees of their respective agencies, and fair and efficient disciplinary systems to maintain those standards of conduct. All agencies shall have an Inspector General who shall report directly to the respective agency head and to the Commissioner of Investigation and be responsible for maintaining standards of conduct as may be established in such agency under this Order. Inspectors General shall be responsible for the investigation and elimination of corrupt or other criminal activity, conflicts of interest, unethical conduct, misconduct, and incompetence within their respective agencies. Except to the extent otherwise provided by law, the employment or continued employment of all existing and prospective Inspectors General and members of their staffs shall be subject to complete background investigations and approval by the Department of Investigation.

1. According to the above passage, establishing written standards of conduct for each agency is the responsibility of the
   A. agency head
   B. Commissioner of Investigation
   C. Department of Investigation
   D. Inspector General

1.____

2. According to the above passage, maintaining standards of conduct within each agency is the responsibility of the
   A. agency head
   B. Commissioner of Investigation
   C. Department of Investigation
   D. Inspector General

2.____

Questions 3-6.

DIRECTIONS: Questions 3 through 6 are to be answered SOLELY on the basis of the information contained in the following passage.

Assume that Warehouse X uses the following procedures for receiving stock. When a delivery is received, the stock handler who receives the delivery should immediately unpack and check the delivery. This check is to ensure that the quantity and kinds of stock items delivered match those on the purchase order which had been sent to the vendor. After the delivery is check, a receiving report is prepared by the same stock handler. This receiving report should include the name of the shipper, the purchase order number, the description of the item, and the actual count or weight of the item. The receiving report, along with the packing slip, should then be checked by the stores clerk against the purchase order to make sure that the quantity received is correct. This is necessary before credit can be obtained from the vendor for any items that are missing or damaged. After the checking is completed, the stock items can be moved to the stockroom.

3. According to the procedures described above, the stock person who receives the delivery should
   A. place the unopened delivery in a secure area for checking at a later date
   B. notify the stores clerk that the delivery has arrived and is ready for checking
   C. unpack the delivery and check the quantity and types of stock items against the purchase order
   D. closely examine the outside of the delivery containers for dents and damages

3._____

4. According to the procedures described above, credit can be obtained from the vendor
   A. *before* the stock handler checks the delivery of stock items
   B. *after* the stock handler checks the delivery of stock items
   C. *before* the stores clerk checks the receiving report against the purchase order
   D. *after* the stores clerk checks the receiving report against the purchase order

4._____

5. According to the procedures described above, all of the following information should be included when filling out a receiving report EXCEPT the
   A. purchase order number   B. name of the shipper
   C. count or weight of the item   D. unit cost per item

5._____

6. According to the procedures described above, after the stores clerk has checked the receiving report against the purchase order, the NEXT step is to
   A. move the stock items to the stockroom
   B. return the stock items received to the vendor
   C. give the stock items to the stock handler for final checking
   D. file the packing slip for inventory purposes

6._____

Questions 7-9.

DIRECTIONS: Questions 7 through 9 are to be answered SOLELY on the basis of the information contained in the following passage.

A filing system for requisition forms used in a warehouse will be of maximum benefit only if it provides ready access to information needed and is not too complex. How effective the system will be depends largely on how well the filing system is organized. A well-organized system usually results in a smooth-running operation.

When setting up a system for filing requisition forms, one effective method would be to first make an alphabetical listing of all the authorized requisitioning agencies. Then file folders should be prepared for each of these agencies and arranged alphabetically in file cabinets. Following this, each agency should be assigned a series of numbers corresponding to those on the blank requisition forms with which they will be supplied. When an agency then submits a requisition and it is filled, the form should be filed in numerical order in the designated agency folder. By using this system, any individual requisition form which is missing from its folder can be easily detected. Regardless of the filing system used, simplicity is essential if the filing system is to be successful.

7. According to the above passage, a filing system is MOST likely to be successful if it is
   A. alphabetical
   B. uncomplicated
   C. numerical
   D. reliable

8. According to the above passage, the reason numbers are assigned to each agency is to
   A. simplify stock issuing procedures
   B. keep a count of all incoming requisition forms
   C. be able to know when a form is missing from its folder
   D. eliminate the need for an alphabetical filing system

9. According to the above passage, which one of the following is an ACCURATE statement regarding the establishment of a well-organized filing system?
   A. Requisitioned stock items will be issued at a faster rate.
   B. Stock items will be stored in storage areas alphabetically arranged.
   C. Information concerning ordered stock items will be easily obtainable.
   D. Maximum productivity can be expected from each employee.

Questions 10-13.

DIRECTIONS: Questions 10 through 13 are to be answered SOLELY on the basis of the information contained in the following passage.

On Tuesday, October 21, Protection Agent Williams, on duty at the Jamaica Depot, observed a man jump over the fence and into the parking lot at 2:12 P.M. and run to a car that was parked with the engine running. The man, who limped slightly, opened the car door, jumped into the car, and sped out of the yard. The car was a 2018 gray Buick Electra, license plate 563-JYN, with parking decal No. 6043. The man was white, about 6 feet tall, about 175 pounds, in his mid-20's, with a scar on his left cheek. He wore a blue sportcoat, tan slacks, a white shift open at the neck with no tie, and brown loafers.

10. What was the color of the car?
    A. White
    B. Blue
    C. Two-tone brown and tan
    D. Gray

11. What were the distinguishing personal features of the man who jumped over 11.____
    the fence?
    A. A scar on the left cheek   B. Pockmarks on his face
    C. A cast on his left wrist   D. Bushy eyebrows

12. What was the number on the car's parking decal? 12.____
    A. 2018   B. 673-JYN   C. 6043   D. 175

13. On what day of the week did the incident occur? 13.____
    A. Monday   B. Tuesday   C. Wednesday   D. Sunday

14. *It is a violation of rules for a Protection Agent to carry a firearm while on* 14.____
    Transit Authority property. The possession of such a weapon, whether carried
    on the person, in a personal vehicle, or stored in a locker, can result in charges
    being filed against the Agent.
    According to the above information, the carrying of a firearm
    A. on Authority property by any employee is prohibited
    B. anywhere by an Agent is prohibited under all circumstances
    C. on Authority property by an Agent is prohibited under all circumstances
    D. anywhere by an Authority employee may be reason for charges being
       filed against that employee

15. *News reporters may enter Authority property if they have the written* 15.____
    authorization of a Public Affairs Department official. The Agent on duty must
    get permission from the Property Protection Control Desk before admitting to
    the property a news person who has no such written authorization.
    If a reporter tells a Protection Agent that she has received permission from the
    Authority President to enter the property, what is the FIRST thing the Agent
    should do?
    A. Call the Authority police.
    B. Admit the reporter immediately.
    C. Call the Authority President's office.
    D. Call the Property Protection Control Desk.

Questions 16-20.

DIRECTIONS: Questions 16 through 20 are to be answered SOLELY on the basis of the
              information contained in the following passage.

FIRES AND EXTINGUISHERS

There are four classes of fires.

Trash fires, paper fires, cloth fires, wood fires, etc. are classified as Class A fires. Water or a water-base solution should be used to extinguish Class A fires. They also can be extinguished by covering the combustibles with a multi-purpose dry chemical.

Burning liquids, gasoline, oil, paint, tar, etc. are considered Class B fires. Such fires can be extinguished by smothering or blanketing them. Extinguishers used for Class B fires are Halon, CO_2, or multi-purpose dry chemical. Water tends to spread such fires and should not be used.

Fires in electrical equipment and switchboards are classified as Class C fires. When live electrical equipment is involved, a non-conducting extinguishing agent like CO_2, a multi-purpose dry chemical, or Halon should always be used. Soda-acid or other water-type extinguishers should not be used.

Class D fires consist of burning metals in finely-divided forms like chips, turnings, and shavings. Specially-designed extinguishing agents that provide a smothering blanket or coating should be used to extinguish Class D fires. Multi-purpose dry-powder extinguishants are such agents.

16. The ONLY type of extinguishing agent that can be used on any type of fire is
    A. a multi-purpose, dry-chemical extinguishing agent
    B. soda-acid
    C. water
    D. carbon dioxide

17. A fire in litter swept from a subway car in a yard is MOST likely to be a Class _____ fire.
    A. A   B. B   C. C   D. D

18. Fire coming from the underbody of a subway car is MOST likely to be a Class _____ fire.
    A. A   B. B   C. C   D. D

19. Which of the following extinguishing agents should NOT be used in fighting a Class C fire involving live electrical equipment?
    A. Halon   B. Carbon dioxide
    C. A multi-purpose dry chemical   D. Soda-acid

20. Water is NOT recommended for use on Class B fires because water
    A. would cool the fire   B. evaporates too quickly
    C. might spread the fire   D. would smother the fire

Questions 21-24.

DIRECTIONS: Questions 21 through 24 are to be answered SOLELY on the basis of the information contained in the following passage.

Protection Agent Brown, working the midnight to 8:00 A.M. tour at the Flushing Bus Depot, discovered a fire at 2:17 A.M. in Bus No. 4651, which was parked in the southeast portion of the depot yard. He turned in an alarm to the Fire Department from Box 3297 on the nearby street at 2:18 A.M. At 2:20 A.M., he called the Property Protection Control Desk and reported the fire and his action to Line Supervisor Wilson. Line Supervisor Wilson instructed Agent Brown to lock his booth and go to the fire alarm box to direct the fire companies. The first arriving companies were Engine 307 and Ladder 154. Brown directed them to the burning bus. Two minutes later, at 2:23 A.M. Battalion Chief Welsh arrived from Battalion 14. The fire had made little headway. It was extinguished in about two minutes. Brown then wrote a fire report for submittal to Line Supervisor Wilson.

21. What was the FIRST thing Protection Agent Brown did after observing the fire? He 21._____
    A. called Battalion Chief Welsh
    B. called the Fire Dispatcher
    C. transmitted an alarm from a nearby alarm box
    D. called 911

22. In what part of the yard was the burning bus? 22._____
    A. Northeast section   B. Southwest end
    C. Northwest part   D. Southeast portion

23. What time did Agent Brown call Line Supervisor Wilson? 23._____
    A. 2:18 P.M.   B. 2:20 A.M.   C. 2:29 A.M.   D. 2:36 A.M.

24. Which of the following CORRECTLY describes the sequence of Agent Brown's actions? He 24._____
    A. saw the fire, turned in an alarm, called the Property Protection Control Desk, directed the fire companies to the fire, and wrote a report
    B. called the Property Protection Control Desk, directed the fire apparatus, directed Chief Welsh, and wrote a report
    C. called Line Supervisor Wilson, turned in an alarm, waited by the burning bus, and directed the fire companies
    D. called Line Supervisor Wilson, directed the firefighters, waited for instructions from Line Supervisor Wilson, and wrote a report

Questions 25-26.

DIRECTIONS: Questions 25 and 26 are to be answered SOLELY on the basis of the information contained in the following passage.

Protection Agents may admit to Transit Authority headquarters only persons with Transit Authority passes, persons with job appointment letters, and persons who have permission to enter from Transit Authority officials.

During his tour in the Authority's headquarters lobby, Protection Agent Williams admitted to the building 326 persons with Authority passes and 41 persons with job appointment letters. He telephoned authorized officials for permission to admit 14 others, 13 of whom were granted permission and entered and one of whom was denied permission. He also turned away two persons who wanted to enter to sell to employees merchandise for their personal use, and one person who appeared inebriated.

25. How many persons did Agent Williams admit to the building? 25.____
    A. 326   B. 367   C. 380   D. 382

26. To how many persons did Agent Williams refuse admittance? 26.____
    A. 4   B. 13   C. 14   D. 41

Questions 27-30.

DIRECTIONS: Questions 27 through 30 are to be answered SOLELY on the basis of the information contained in the following instructions on Lost Property.

LOST PROPERTY

All inquiries for information regarding lost property will be referred to the Lost Property Office. Any Station Department employee finding a lost article, of any description, will immediately hand it over to the railroad clerk in the nearest 24-hour booth of the station where the article is found. The clerk must give the employee a receipt for the article. Should a passenger hand over a lost article to a cleaner, the cleaner will offer to escort the passenger to the nearest 24-hour booth in order that a receipt may be given by the railroad clerk there. If the passenger declines, the cleaner will accept the lost article without giving a receipt and proceed as desired above. Each employee who receive lost property will be held responsible for it unless he produces a receipt for it from another employee. Should any lost property disappear, the last employee who signed for it will be held accountable.

27. If a cleaner turns in a lost article to a railroad clerk in the nearest 24-hour booth, 27.____
    he should make sure that he
    A. gets a receipt for the article
    B. notifies his supervisor about the lost article
    C. finds out the name of the owner of the article
    D. writes a report on the incident

28. If a lost article disappears after a cleaner has properly turned it in to the 28.____
    railroad clerk in the nearest 24-hour booth, the one who will be held
    accountable is the
    A. person who found the lost article
    B. cleaner who turned in the article
    C. supervisor in charge of the station
    D. last employee to sign a receipt for the article

29. A passenger finds a lost article and gives it to a cleaner. The cleaner gives the 29.____
    passenger a receipt.
    The cleaner's action was
    A. *proper*, because the passenger was relieved of any responsibility for the lost article
    B. *improper*, because the cleaner should have offered to escort the passenger to the nearest 24-hour booth
    C. *proper*, because the cleaner is required to give the passenger a receipt
    D. *improper*, because the cleaner should have sent the passenger to the Lost Property Office

8 (#2)

30. A cleaner finds a five dollar bill on a crowded station platform. Three passengers who see him pick it up rush up and claim the money. The first passenger said he had just taken a roll of bills out of his pocket and must have dropped it. The second said he had just given two five dollar bills to his wife, and she had dropped one of them. The third said he had a hole in his pocket and the bill fell out of it.
The cleaner should
- A. give the five dollar bill t the second passenger because he had his wife as a witness
- B. give the five dollar bill to the third passenger because he had a hole in his pocket
- C. keep the five dollar bill
- D. bring the five dollar bill to the railroad clerk in the nearest 24-hour booth

30._____

KEY (CORRECT ANSWERS)

1.	A	11.	A	21.	C
2.	D	12.	C	22.	D
3.	C	13.	B	23.	B
4.	D	14.	C	24.	A
5.	D	15.	D	25.	C
6.	A	16.	A	26.	A
7.	B	17.	A	27.	A
8.	C	18.	C	28.	D
9.	C	19.	D	29.	B
10.	D	20.	C	30.	D

REPORT WRITING
EXAMINATION SECTION
TEST 1

DIRECTIONS: Each question or incomplete statement is followed by several suggested answers or completions. Select the one that BEST answers the question or completes the statement. *PRINT THE LETTER OF THE CORRECT ANSWER IN THE SPACE AT THE RIGHT.*

1. Following are six steps that should be taken in the course of report preparation:
   I. Outlining the material for presentation in the report
   II. Analyzing and interpreting the facts
   III. Analyzing the problem
   IV. Reaching conclusions
   V. Writing, revising, and rewriting the final copy
   VI. Collecting data

   According to the principles of good report writing, the CORRECT order in which these steps should be taken is:
   A. VI, III, II, I, IV, V
   B. III, VI, II, IV, I, V
   C. III, VI, II, I, IV, V
   D. VI, II, III, IV, I, V

   1.____

2. Following are three statements concerning written reports:
   I. Clarity is generally more essential in oral reports than in written reports.
   II. Short sentences composed of simple words are generally preferred to complex sentences and difficult words.
   III. Abbreviations may be used whenever they are customary and will not distract the attention of the reader.

   Which of the following choices correctly classifies the above statements in to those which are valid and those which are not valid?
   A. I and II are valid, but III is not valid
   B. I is valid, but II and III are not valid.
   C. II and III are valid, but I is not valid.
   D. III is valid, but I and II are not valid.

   2.____

3. In order to produce a report written in a style that is both understandable and effective, an investigator should apply the principles of unit, coherence, and emphasis.
   The one of the following which is the BEST example of the principle of coherence is
   A. interlinking sentences so that thoughts flow smoothly
   B. having each sentence express a single idea to facilitate comprehension
   C. arranging important points in prominent positions so they are not overlooked
   D. developing the main idea fully to insure complete consideration

   3.____

4. Assume that a supervisor is preparing a report recommending that a standard work procedure be changed.
   Of the following, the MOST important information that he should include in this report is
   A. a complete description of the present procedure
   B. the details and advantages of the recommended procedure
   C. the type and amount of retraining needed
   D. the percentage of men who favor the change

5. When you include in your report on an inspection some information which you have obtained from other individuals, it is MOST important that
   A. this information have no bearing on the work these other people are performing
   B. you do not report as fact the opinions of other individuals
   C. you keep the source of the information confidential
   D. you do not tell the other individuals that their statements will be included in your report

6. Before turning in a report of an investigator of an accident, you discover some additional information you did not know about when you wrote the report.
   Whether or not you re-write your report to include this additional information should depend MAINLY on the
   A. source of this additional information
   B. established policy covering the subject matter of the report
   C. length of the report and the time it would take you to re-write it
   D. bearing this additional information will have on the conclusions in the report

7. The MOST desirable *first* step in the planning of a written report is to
   A. ascertain what necessary information is readily available in the files
   B. outline the methods you will employ to get the necessary information
   C. determine the objectives and uses of the report
   D. estimate the time and cost required to complete the report

8. In writing a report, the practice of taking up the least important points and the most important points last is a
   A. *good* technique since the final points made in a report will make the greatest impression on the reader
   B. *good* technique since the material is presented in a more logical manner and will lead directly to the conclusions
   C. *poor* technique since the reader's time is wasted by having to review irrelevant information before finishing the report
   D. *poor* technique since it may cause the reader to lose interest in the report and arrive at incorrect conclusions about the report

9. Which one of the following serves as the BEST guideline for you to follow for effective written reports?
Keep sentences
   A. short and limit sentences to one thought
   B. short and use as many thoughts as possible
   C. long and limit sentences to one thought
   D. long and use as many thoughts as possible

9.____

10. One method by which a supervisor might prepare written reports to management is to begin with the conclusions, results, or summary, and to follow this with the supporting data.
The BEST reason why management may *prefer* this form of report is that
   A. management lacks the specific training to understand the data
   B. the data completely supports the conclusions
   C. time is saved by getting to the conclusions of the report first
   D. the data contains all the information that is required for making the conclusions

10.____

11. When making written reports, it is MOST important that they be
   A. well-worded   B. accurate as to the facts
   C. brief   D. submitted immediately

11.____

12. Of the following, the MOST important reason for a supervisor to prepare good written reports is that
   A. a supervisor is rated on the quality of his reports
   B. decisions are often made on the basis of the reports
   C. such reports take less time for superiors to review
   D. such reports demonstrate efficiency of department operations

12.____

13. Of the following, the BEST test of a good report is whether it
   A. provides the information needed
   B. shows the good sense of the writer
   C. is prepared according to a proper format
   D. is grammatical and neat

13.____

14. When a supervisor writes a report, he can BEST show that he has a understanding of the subject of the report by
   A. including necessary facts and omitting nonessential details
   B. using statistical data
   C. giving his conclusions but not the data on which they are based
   D. using a technical vocabulary

14.____

15. Suppose you and another supervisor on the same level are assigned to work together on a report. You disagree strongly with one of the recommendations the other supervisor wants to include in the report but you cannot change his views.

15.____

Of the following, it would be BEST that
- A. you refuse to accept responsibility for the report
- B. you ask that someone else be assigned to this project to replace you
- C. each of you state his own ideas about this recommendation in the report
- D. you give in to the other supervisor's opinion for the sake of harmony

16. Standardized forms are often provided for submitting reports.
Of the following, the MOST important advantage of using standardized forms for reports is that
    - A. they take less time to prepare than individually written reports
    - B. the person making the report can omit information he considers unimportant
    - C. the responsibility for preparing these reports can be turned over to subordinates
    - D. necessary information is less likely to be omitted

17. A report which may BEST be classed as a *periodic* report is one which
    - A. requires the same type of information at regular intervals
    - B. contains detailed information which is to be retained in permanent records
    - C. is prepared whenever a special situation occurs
    - D. lists information in graphic form

18. In the writing of reports or letters, the ideas presented in a paragraph are usually of unequal importance and require varying degrees of emphasis.
All of the following are methods of placing extra stress on an idea EXCEPT
    - A. repeating it in a number of forms
    - B. placing it in the middle of the paragraph
    - C. placing it either at the beginning or at the end of a paragraph
    - D. underlining it

Questions 19-25.

DIRECTIONS: Questions 19 through 25 concern the subject of report writing and are based on the information and incidents described in the following paragraph. (In answering these questions, assume that the facts and incidents in the paragraph are true.)

On December 15, at 8 A.M., seven Laborers reported to Foreman Joseph Meehan in the Greenbranch Yard in Queens. Meehan instructed the men to load some 50-pound boxes of books on a truck for delivery to an agency building in Brooklyn. Meehan told the men that, because the boxes were rather heavy, two men should work together, helping each other lift and load each box. Since Michael Harper, one of the Laborers, was without a partner, Meehan helped him with the boxes for a while. When Meehan was called to the telephone in a nearby building, however, Harper decided to lift a box himself. He appeared able to lift the box, but, as he got the box halfway up, he cried out that he had a sharp pain in his back. Another Laborer, Jorge Ortiz, who was passing by, ran over to help Harper put the box down. Harper suddenly dropped the box, which fell on Ortiz' right foot. By this time, Meehan had come out of the building. He immediately helped get the box off Ortiz' foot and had both men lie down. Meehan covered the men with blankets and called an ambulance, which arrived a half hour later. At the hospital, the doctor said that the X-ray results showed that Ortiz' right foot was broken in three places.

19. What would be the BEST term to use in a report describing the injury of Jorge Ortiz?
    A. Strain   B. Fracture   C. Hernia   D. Hemorrhage

19.____

20. Which of the following would be the MOST accurate summary for the Foreman to put in his report of the incident?
    A. Ortiz attempted to help Harper carry a box which was too heavy for one person, but Harper dropped it before Ortiz got there.
    B. Ortiz tried to help Harper carry a box but Harper got a pain in his back and accidentally dropped the box on Ortiz' foot.
    C. Harper refused to follow Meehan's orders and lifted a box too heavy for him; he deliberately dropped it when Ortiz tried to help him carry it.
    D. Harper lifted a box and felt a pain in his back; Ortiz tried to help Harper put the box down but Harper accidentally dropped it on Ortiz' foot.

20.____

21. One of the Laborers at the scene of the accident was asked his version of the incident.
Which information obtained from this witness would be LEAST important for including in the accident report?
    A. His opinion as to the cause of the accident
    B. How much of the accident he saw
    C. His personal opinion of the victims
    D. His name and address

21.____

22. What should be the MAIN objective of writing a report about the incident described in the above paragraph? To
    A. describe the important elements in the accident situation
    B. recommend that such Laborers as Ortiz be advised not to interfere in another's work unless given specific instructions
    C. analyze the problems occurring when there are not enough workers to perform a certain task
    D. illustrate the hazards involved in performing routine everyday tasks

22.____

23. Which of the following is information *missing* from the above passage but which *should* be included in a report of the incident? The
    A. name of the Laborer's immediate supervisor
    B. contents of the boxes
    C. time at which the accident occurred
    D. object or action that caused the injury to Ortiz' foot

23.____

24. According to the description of the incident, the accident occurred because
    A. Ortiz attempted to help Harper who resisted his help
    B. Harper failed to follow instructions given him by Meehan
    C. Meehan was not supervising his men as closely as he should have
    D. Harper was not strong enough to carry the box once he lifted it

24.____

25. Which of the following is MOST important for a foreman to avoid when writing up an official accident report? 25.____
    A. Using technical language to describe equipment involved in the accident
    B. Putting in details which might later be judged unnecessary
    C. Giving an opinion as to conditions that contributed to the accident
    D. Recommending discipline for employees who, in his opinion, caused the accident

KEY (CORRECT ANSWERS)

1.	B	11.	B
2.	C	12.	B
3.	A	13.	A
4.	B	14.	A
5.	B	15.	C
6.	D	16.	D
7.	C	17.	A
8.	D	18.	B
9.	A	19.	B
10.	C	20.	D

21. C
22. A
23. C
24. B
25. D

TEST 2

DIRECTIONS: Each question or incomplete statement is followed by several suggested answers or completions. Select the one that BEST answers the question or completes the statement. *PRINT THE LETTER OF THE CORRECT ANSWER IN THE SPACE AT THE RIGHT.*

1. Lieutenant X is preparing a report to submit to his commanding officer in order to get approval of a plan of operation he has developed.
   The report starts off with the statement of the problem and continues with the details of the problem. It contains factual information gathered with the help of field and operational personnel. It contains a final conclusion and recommendation for action. The recommendation is supplemented by comments from other precinct staff members on how the recommendations will affect their areas of responsibility. The report also includes directives and general orders ready for the commanding officer's signature. In addition, it has two statements of objections presented by two precinct staff members.
   Which one of the following, if any, is either an item that Lieutenant X should have included in his report and which is not mentioned above, or is an item which Lieutenant X improperly did include in his report?
   A. Considerations of alternative courses of action and their consequences should have been covered in the report.
   B. The additions containing undocumented objections to the recommended course of action should not have been included as part of the report.
   C. A statement on the qualifications of Lieutenant X, which would support his expertness in the field under consideration, should have been included in the report.
   D. The directives and general orders should not have been prepared and included in the report until the commanding officer had approved the recommendations.
   E. None of the above, since Lieutenant X's report was both proper and complete.

1._____

2. During a visit to a section, the district supervisor criticizes the method being used by the assistant foreman to prepare a certain report and orders him to modify the method. This change ordered by the district supervisor is in direct conflict with the specific orders of the foreman.
   In this situation, it would be BEST for the assistant foreman to
   A. change the method and tell the foreman about the change at the first opportunity
   B. change the method and rely on the district supervisor to notify the foreman
   C. report the matter to the foreman and delay the preparation of the report
   D. ask the district supervisor to discuss the matter with the foreman but use the old method for the time being

2._____

3. A department officer should realize that the MOST usual reason for writing a report is to
   A. give orders and follow up their execution
   B. establish a permanent record
   C. raise questions
   D. supply information

4. A very important report which is being prepared by a department officer will soon be due on the desk of the district supervisor. No typing help is available at this time for the officer.
   For the officer to write out this report in longhand in such a situation would be
   A. *bad*; such a report would not make the impression a typed report would
   B. *good*; it is important to get the report in on time
   C. *bad*; the district supervisor should not be required to read longhand reports
   D. *good*; it would call attention to the difficult conditions under which this section must work

5. In a well-written report, the length of each paragraph in the report should be
   A. varied according to the content
   B. not over 300 words
   C. pretty nearly the same
   D. gradually longer as the report is developed and written

6. A clerk in the headquarters office complains to you about the way in which you are filing out a certain report.
   It would be BEST for you to
   A. tell the clerk that you are following official procedures in filling out the report
   B. ask to be referred to the clerk's superior
   C. ask the clerk exactly what is wrong with the way in which you are filling out the report
   D. tell the clerk that you are following the directions of the district supervisor

7. The use of an outline to help in writing a report is
   A. *desirable*, in order to insure good organization and coverage
   B. *necessary*, so it can be used as an introduction to the report itself
   C. *undesirable*, since it acts as a straightjacket and may result in an unbalanced report
   D. *desirable*, if you know your immediate supervisor reads reports with extreme care and attention

8. It is advisable that a department officer do his paper work and report writing as soon as he has completed an inspection MAINLY because
   A. there are usually deadlines to be met
   B. it insures a steady work-flow
   C. he may not have time for this later
   D. the facts are then freshest in his mind

9. Before you turn in a report you have written of an investigation that you have made, you discover some additional information you didn't know about before. Whether or not you re-write the report to include this additional information should depend MAINLY on the
    A. amount of time remaining before the report is due
    B. established policy of the department covering the subject matter of the report
    C. bearing this information will have on the conclusions of the report
    D. number of people who will eventually review the report

9.____

10. When a supervisory officer submits a periodic report to the district supervisor, he should realize that the CHIEF importance of such a report is that it
    A. is the principal method of checking on the efficiency of the supervisor and his subordinates
    B. is something to which frequent reference will be made
    C. eliminates the need for any personal follow-up or inspection by higher echelons
    D. permits the district supervisor to exercise his functions of direction, supervision, and control better

10.____

11. Conclusions and recommendations are usually placed at the end rather than at the beginning of a report because
    A. the person preparing the report may decide to change some of the conclusions and recommendations before he reaches the end of the report
    B. they are the most important part of the report
    C. they can be judged better by the person to whom the report is sent after he reads the facts and investigators which come earlier in the report
    D. they can be referred to quickly when needed without reading the rest of the report

11.____

12. The use of the same method of record-keeping and reporting by all agency sections is
    A. *desirable*, MAINLY because it saves time in section operations
    B. *undesirable*, MAINLY because it kills the initiative of the individual section foreman
    C. *desirable*, MAINLY because it will be easier for the administrator to evaluate and compare section operations
    D. *undesirable*, MAINLY because operations vary from section to section and uniform record-keeping and reporting is not appropriate

12.____

13. The GREATEST benefit the section officer will have from keeping complete and accurate records and reports of section operations is that
    A. he will find it easier to run his section efficiently
    B. he will need less equipment
    C. he will need less manpower
    D. the section will run smoothly when he is out

13.____

14. You have prepared a report to your superior and are ready to send it forward. But on re-reading it, you think some parts are not clearly expressed and your superior ay have difficulty getting your point.
    Of the following, it would be BEST for you to
    A. give the report to one of your men to read, and if he has no trouble understanding it send it through
    B. forward the report and call your superior the next day to ask whether it was all right
    C. forward the report as is; higher echelons should be able to understand any report prepared by a section officer
    D. do the report over, re-writing the sections you are in doubt about

15. The BEST of the following statements concerning reports is that
    A. a carelessly written report may give the reader an impression of inaccuracy
    B. correct grammar and English are unimportant if the main facts are given
    C. every man should be required to submit a daily work report
    D. the longer and more wordy a report is, the better it will read

16. In writing a report, the question of whether or not to include certain material could be determined BEST by considering the
    A. amount of space the material will occupy in the report
    B. amount of time to be spent in gathering the material
    C. date of the material
    D. value of the material to the superior who will read the report

17. Suppose you are submitting a fairly long report to your superior.
    The one of the following sections that should come FIRST in this report is a
    A. description of how you gathered material
    B. discussion of possible objections to your recommendations
    C. plan of how your recommendations can be put into practice
    D. statement of the problem dealt with

Questions 18-20.

DIRECTIONS: A foreman is asked to write a report on the incident described in the following passage. Answer Questions 18 through 20 based on the following information.

On March 10, Henry Moore, a laborer, was in the process of transferring some equipment from the machine shop to the third floor. He was using a dolly to perform this task and, as he was wheeling the material through the machine shop, laborer Bob Greene called to him. As Henry turned to respond to Bob, he jammed the dolly into Larry Mantell's leg, knocking Larry down in the process and causing the heavy drill that Larry was holding to fall on Larry's foot. Larry started rubbing his foot and then, infuriated, jumped up and punched Henry in the jaw. The force of the blow drove Henry's head back against the wall. Henry did not fight back; he appeared to be dazed. An ambulance was called to take Henry to the hospital, and the ambulance attendant told the foreman that it appeared likely that Henry had suffered a concussion. Larry's injuries consisted of some bruises, but he refused medical attention.

18. An adequate report of the above incident should give as minimum information the names of the persons involved, the names of the witnesses, the date and the time that each event took place, and the   18.____
    A. names of the ambulance attendants
    B. names of all the employees working in the machine shop
    C. location where the accident occurred
    D. nature of the previous safety training each employee had been given

19. The only one of the following which is NOT a fact is   19.____
    A. Bob called to Henry
    B. Larry suffered a concussion
    C. Larry rubbed his foot
    D. the incident took place in the machine shop

20. Which of the following would be the MOST accurate summary of the incident for the foreman to put in his report of the accident?   20.____
    A. Larry Mantell punched Henry Moore because a drill fell on his foot and he was angry. Then Henry fell and suffered a concussion.
    B. Henry Moore accidentally jammed a dolly into Larry Mantell's foot, knocking Larry down. Larry punched Henry, pushing him into the wall and causing him to bang his head against the wall.
    C. Bob Greene called Henry Moore. A dolly than jammed into Larry Mantell and knocked him down. Larry punched Henry who tripped and suffered some bruises. An ambulance was called.
    D. A drill fell on Larry Mantell's foot. Larry jumped up suddenly and punched Henry Moore and pushed him into the wall. Henry may have suffered a concussion as a result of falling.

Questions 21-25.

DIRECTIONS: Questions 21 through 25 are to be answered ONLY on the basis of the information provided in the following passage.

A written report is a communication of information from one person to another. It is an account of some matter especially investigated, however routine that matter may be. The ultimate basis of any good written report is facts, which become known through observation and verification. Good written reports may seem to be no more than general ideas and opinions. However, in such cases, the facts leading to these opinions were gathered, verified, and reported earlier, and the opinions are dependent upon these facts. Good style, proper form, and emphasis cannot make a good written report out of unreliable information and bad judgment; but, on the other hand, solid investigation and brilliant thinking are not likely to become very useful until they are effectively communicated to others. If a person's work calls for written reports, then his work is often no better than his written reports.

21. Based on the information in the above passage, it can be concluded that opinions expressed in a report should be
    A. based on facts which are gathered and reported
    B. emphasized repeatedly when they result from a special investigation
    C. kept to a minimum
    D. separated from the body of the report

    21._____

22. In the above passage, the one of the following which is mentioned as a way of establishing facts is
    A. authority
    B. communication
    C. reporting
    D. verification

    22._____

23. According to the above passage, the characteristic shared by ALL written reports is that they are
    A. accounts of routine matters
    B. transmissions of information
    C. reliable and logical
    D. written in proper form

    23._____

24. Which of the following conclusions can logically be drawn from the information given in the above passage?
    A. Brilliant thinking can make up for unreliable information in a report.
    B. One method of judging an individual's work is the quality of the written reports he is required to submit.
    C. Proper form and emphasis can make a good report out of unreliable information.
    D. Good written reports that seem to be no more than general ideas should be rewritten.

    24._____

25. Which of the following suggested titles would be MOST appropriate for this passage?
    A. Gathering and Organizing Facts
    B. Techniques of Observation
    C. Nature and Purpose of Reports
    D. Reports and Opinions: Differences and Similarities

    25._____

KEY (CORRECT ANSWERS)

1.	A	11.	C
2.	A	12.	C
3.	D	13.	A
4.	B	14.	D
5.	A	15.	A
6.	C	16.	D
7.	A	17.	D
8.	D	18.	C
9.	C	19.	B
10.	D	20.	B

21. A
22. D
23. B
24. B
25. C

TEST 3

DIRECTIONS: Each question or incomplete statement is followed by several suggested answers or completions. Select the one that BEST answers the question or completes the statement. *PRINT THE LETTER OF THE CORRECT ANSWER IN THE SPACE AT THE RIGHT.*

Questions 1-5.

DIRECTIONS: The following is an accident report similar to those used in departments for reporting accidents. Questions 1 through 5 are be answered using ONLY the information given in this report.

ACCIDENT REPORT

FROM: John Doe	**DATE OF REPORT:** June 23	
TITLE: Sanitation Worker		
DATE OF ACCIDENT: June 22 time 3 ~~AM~~ PM	**CITY:** Metropolitan	
PLACE: 1489 Third Avenue		
VEHICLE NO. 1	**VEHICLE NO. 2**	
OPERATOR: John Doe, <u>Sanitation Worker</u> Title	**OPERATOR:** Richard Roe	
VEHICLE CODE NO: 14-238	**ADDRESS:** 498 High Street	
LICENSE NO.: 0123456	**OWNER:** Henry Roe **ADDRESS:** 786 E.83 St.	**LIC. NO.:** 5N1492
DESCRIPTION OF ACCIDENT: Light green Chevrolet sedan while trying to pass drove in to rear side of sanitation truck which had stopped to collect garbage. No one was injured but there was property damage.		
NATURE OF DAMAGE TO PRIVATE VEHICLE: Right front fender crushed, bumper bent		
DAMAGE TO CITY VEHICLE: Front of left rear fender pushed in. Paint scraped.		
NAME OF WITNESS: Frank Brown	**ADDRESS:** 48 Kingsway	
SIGNATURE OF PERSON MAKING THIS REPORT *John Doe*	**BADGE NO.:** 428	

1. Of the following, the one which has been omitted from this accident report is the 1.____
   A. location of the accident
   B. drivers of the vehicles involved
   C. traffic situation at the time of the accident
   D. owners of the vehicles involved

2. The address of the driver of Vehicle No. 1 is not required because he 2.____
   A. is employed by the department
   B. is not the owner of the vehicle
   C. reported the accident
   D. was injured in the accident

3. The report indicates that the driver of Vehicle No. 2 was PROBABLY 3.____
   A. passing on the wrong side of the truck
   B. not wearing his glasses
   C. not injured in the accident
   D driving while intoxicated

4. The number of people *specifically* referred to in this report is 4.____
   A. 3 B. 4 C. 5 D. 6

5. The license number of Vehicle No. 1 is 5.____
   A. 428 B. 5N1492 C. 14-238 D. 0123456

6. In a report of unlawful entry into department premises, it is LEAST important to include the 6.____
   A. estimated value of the property missing
   B. general description of the premises
   C. means used to get into the premises
   D. time and date of entry

7. In a report of an accident, it is LEAST important to include the 7.____
   A. name of the insurance company of the person injured in the accident
   B. probable cause of the accident
   C. time and place of the accident
   D. names and addresses of all witnesses of the accident

8. Of the following, the one which is NOT required in the preparation of a weekly functional expense report is the 8.____
   A. hourly distribution of the time by proper heading in accordance with the actual work performed
   B. signatures of officers not involved in the preparation of the report
   C. time records of the men who appear on the payroll of the respective locations
   D. time records of men working in other districts assigned to this location

KEY (CORRECT ANSWERS)

1.	C	5.	D
2.	A	6.	B
3.	C	7.	A
4.	B	8.	B

PREPARING WRITTEN MATERIAL

PARAGRAPH REARRANGEMENT
COMMENTARY

The sentences that follow are in scrambled order. You are to rearrange them in proper order and indicate the letter choice containing the correct answer at the space at the right.

Each group of sentences in this section is actually a paragraph presented in scrambled order. Each sentence in the group has a place in that paragraph; no sentence is to be left out. You are to read each group of sentences and decide upon the best order in which to put the sentences so as to form a well-organized paragraph.

The questions in this section measure the ability to solve a problem when all the facts relevant to its solution are not given.

More specifically, certain positions of responsibility and authority require the employee to discover connection between events sometimes, apparently, unrelated. In order to do this, the employee will find it necessary to correctly infer that unspecified events have probably occurred or are likely to occur. This ability becomes especially important when action must be taken on incomplete information.

Accordingly, these questions require competitors to choose among several suggested alternatives, each of which presents a different sequential arrangement of the events. Competitors must choose the MOST logical of the suggested sequences.

In order to do so, they may be required to draw on general knowledge to infer missing concepts or events that are essential to sequencing the given events. Competitors should be careful to infer only what is essential to the sequence. The plausibility of the wrong alternatives will always require the inclusion of unlikely events or of additional chains of events which are NOT essential to sequencing the given events.

It's very important to remember that you are looking for the best of the four possible choices, and that the best choice of all may not even be one of the answers you're given to choose from.

There is no one right way to solve these problems. Many people have found it helpful to first write out the order of the sentences, as they would have arranged them, on their scrap paper before looking at the possible answers. If their optimum answer is there, this can save them some time. If it isn't, this method can still give insight into solving the problem. Others find it most helpful to just go through each of the possible choices, contrasting each as they go along. You should use whatever method feels comfortable and works for you.

While most of these types of questions are not that difficult, we've added a higher percentage of the difficult type, just to give you more practice. Usually there are only one or two questions on this section that contain such subtle distinctions that you're unable to answer confidently. And you then may find yourself stuck deciding between two possible choices, neither of which you're sure about.

EXAMINATION SECTION
TEST 1

DIRECTIONS: Each question consists of several sentences which can be arranged in a logical sequence. For each question, select the choice which places the numbered sentences in the MOST logical sequence. *PRINT THE LETTER OF THE CORRECT ANSWER IN THE SPACE AT THE RIGHT.*

1.
   I. A body was found in the woods.
   II. A man proclaimed innocence.
   III. The owner of a gun was located.
   IV. A gun was traced.
   V. The owner of a gun was questioned.
   The CORRECT answer is:
   A. IV, III, V, II, I
   B. II, I, IV, III, V
   C. I, IV, III, V, II
   D. I, III, V, II, IV
   E. I, II, IV, III, V

   1.____

2.
   I. A man is in a hunting accident.
   II. A man fell down a flight of steps.
   III. A man lost his vision in one eye.
   IV. A man broke his leg.
   V. A man had to walk with a cane.
   The CORRECT answer is:
   A. II, IV, V, I, III
   B. IV, V, I, III, II
   C. III, I, IV, V, II
   D. I, III, V, II, IV
   E. I, III, II, IV, V

   2.____

3.
   I. A man is offered a new job.
   II. A woman is offered a new job.
   III. A man works as a waiter.
   IV. A woman works as a waitress.
   V. A woman gives notice.
   The CORRECT answer is:
   A. IV, II, V, III, I
   B. IV, II, V, I, III
   C. II, IV, V, III, I
   D. III, I, IV, II, V
   E. IV, III, II, V, I

   3.____

4.
   I. A train let the station late.
   II. A man was late for work.
   III. A man lost his job.
   IV. Many people complained because the train was late.
   V. There was a traffic jam.
   The CORRECT answer is:
   A. V, II, I, IV, III
   B. V, I, IV, II, III
   C. V, I, II, IV, III
   D. I, V, IV, II, III
   E. II, I, IV, V, III

   4.____

5. I. The burden of proof as to each issue is determined before trial and remains upon the same party throughout the trial.
    II. The jury is at liberty to believe one witness' testimony as against a number of contradictory witnesses.
    III. In a civil case, the party bearing the burden of proof is required to prove his contention by a fair preponderance of the evidence.
    IV. However, it must be noted that a fair preponderance of evidence does not necessarily mean a greater number of witnesses.
    V. The burden of proof is the burden which rests upon one of the parties to an action to persuade the trier of the facts, generally the jury, that a proposition he asserts is true.
    VI. If the evidence is equally balanced, or if it leaves the jury in such doubt as to be unable to decide the controversy either way, judgment must be given against the party upon whom the burden of proof rests.
    The CORRECT answer is:
    A. III, II, V, IV, I, VI B. I, II, VI, V, III, IV C. III, IV, V, I, II, VI
    D. V, I, III, VI, IV, II E. I, V, III, VI, IV, II

6. I. If a parent is without assets and is unemployed, he cannot be convicted of the crime of non-support of a child.
    II. The term *sufficient ability* has been held to mean sufficient financial ability.
    III. It does not matter if his unemployment is by choice or unavoidable circumstances.
    IV. If he fails to take any steps at all, he may be liable to prosecution for endangering the welfare of a child.
    V. Under the penal law, a parent is responsible for the support of his minor child only if the parent is of *sufficient ability*.
    VI. An indigent parent may meet his obligation by borrowing money or by seeking aid under the provisions of the Social Welfare Law.
    The CORRECT answer is:
    A. VI, I, V, III, II, IV B. I, III, V, II, IV, VI C. V, II, I, III, VI, IV
    D. I, VI, IV, V, II, III E. II, V, I, III, VI, IV

7. I. Consider, for example, the case of a rabble rouser who urges a group of twenty people to go out and break the windows of a nearby factory.
    II. Therefore, the law fills the indicated gap with the crime of *inciting to riot*.
    III. A person is considered guilty of inciting to riot when he urges ten or more persons to engage in tumultuous and violent conduct of a kind likely to create public alarm.
    IV. However, if he has not obtained the cooperation of at least four people, he cannot be charged with unlawful assembly.
    V. The charge of inciting to riot was added to the law to cover types of conduct which cannot be classified as either the crime of *riot* or the crime of *unlawful assembly*.
    VI. If he acquires the acquiescence of at least four of them, he is guilty of unlawful assembly even if the project does not materialize.
    The CORRECT answer is:
    A. III, V, I, VI, IV, II B. V, I, IV, VI, II, III C. III, IV, I, V, II, VI
    D. V, I, IV, VI, III, II E. V, III, I, VI, IV, II

8. I. If, however, the rebuttal evidence presents an issue of credibility, it is for the jury to determine whether the presumption has, in fact, been destroyed.
    II. Once sufficient evidence to the contrary is introduced, the presumption disappears from the trial.
    III. The effect of a presumption is to place the burden upon the adversary to come forward with evidence to rebut the presumption.
    IV. When a presumption is overcome and ceases to exist in the case, the fact or facts which gave rise to the presumption still remain.
    V. Whether a presumption has been overcome is ordinarily a question for the court.
    VI. Such information may furnish a basis for a logical inference.
    The CORRECT answer is:
    A. IV, VI, II, V, I, III   B. III, II, V, I, IV, VI   C. V, III, VI, IV, II, I
    D. V, IV, I, II, VI, III   E. II, III, V, I, IV, VI

9. I. An executive may answer a letter by writing his reply on the face of the letter itself instead of having a return letter typed.
    II. This procedure is efficient because it saves the executive's time, the typist's time, and saves office file space.
    III. Copying machines are used in small offices as well as large offices to save time and money in making brief replies to business letters.
    IV. A copy is made on a copying machine to go into the company files, while the original is mailed back to the sender.
    The CORRECT answer is:
    A. I, II, IV, III   B. I, IV, II, III   C. III, I, IV, II   D. III, IV, II, I

10. I. Most organizations favor one of the types but always include the others to a lesser degree.
    II. However, we can detect a definite trend toward greater use of symbolic control.
    III. We suggest that our local police agencies are today primarily utilizing material control.
    IV. Control can be classified into three types: physical, material, and symbolic.
    The CORRECT answer is:
    A. IV, II, III, I   B. II, I, IV, III   C. III, IV, II, I   D. IV, I, III, II

11. I. Project residents had first claim to this use, followed by surrounding neighborhood children.
    II. By contrast, recreation space within the project's interior was found to be used more often by both groups.
    III. Studies of the use of project grounds in many cities showed grounds left open for public use were neglected and unused, both by residents and by members of the surrounding community.
    IV. Project residents had clearly laid claim to the play spaces, setting up and enforcing unwritten rules for use.
    V. Each group, by experience, found their activities easily disrupted by other groups, and their claim to the use of space for recreation difficult to enforce.

The CORRECT answer is:
A. IV, V, I, II, III
B. V, II, IV, III, I
C. I, IV, III, II, V
D. III, V, II, IV, I

12. I. They do not consider the problems correctable within the existing subsidy formula and social policy of accepting all eligible applicants regardless of social behavior.
II. A recent survey, however, indicated that tenants believe these problems correctable by local housing authorities and management within the existing financial formula.
III. Many of the problems and complaints concerning public housing management and design have created resentment between the tenant and the landlord.
IV. This same survey indicated that administrators and managers do not agree with the tenants.
The CORRECT answer is:
A. II, I, III, IV B. I, III, IV, II C. III, II, IV, I D. IV, II, I, III

12.____

13. I. In single-family residences, there is usually enough distance between tenants to prevent occupants from annoying one another.
II. For example, a certain small percentage of tenant families has one or more members addicted to alcohol.
III. While managers believe in the right of individuals to live as they choose, the manager becomes concerned when the pattern of living jeopardizes others' rights.
IV. Still others turn night into day, staging lusty entertainments which carry on into the hours when most tenants are trying to sleep.
V. In apartment buildings, however, tenants live so closely together that any misbehavior can result in unpleasant living conditions.
VI. Other families engage in violent argument.
The CORRECT answer is:
A. III, II, V, IV, VI, I
B. I, V, II, VI, IV, III
C. II, V, IV, I, III, VI
D. IV, II, V, VI, III, I

13.____

14. I. Congress made the commitment explicit in the Housing Act of 194, establishing as a national goal the realization of a *decent home and suitable environment for every American family*.
II. The result has been that the goal of decent home and suitable environment is still as far distant as ever for the disadvantaged urban family.
III. In spite of this action by Congress, federal housing programs have continued to be fragmented and grossly underfunded.
IV. The passage of the National Housing Act signaled a few federal commitment to provide housing for the nation's citizens.
The CORRECT answer is:
A. I, IV, III, II B. IV, I, III, II C. IV, I, II, III D. II, IV, I, III

14.____

15.
I. The greater expense does not necessarily involve *exploitation*, but it is often perceived as exploitative and unfair by those who are aware of the price differences involved, but unaware of operating costs.
II. Ghetto residents believe they are *exploited* by local merchants, and evidence substantiates some of these beliefs.
III. However, stores in low-income areas were more likely to be small independents, which could not achieve the economies available to supermarket chains and were, therefore, more likely to charge higher prices, and the customers were more likely to buy smaller-sized packages which are more expensive per unit of measure.
IV. A study conducted in one city showed that distinctly higher prices were charged for goods sold in ghetto stores in other areas.
The CORRECT answer is:
  A. IV, II, I, III   B. IV, I, III, II   C. II, IV, III, I   D. II, III, IV, I

15.____

KEY (CORRECT ANSWERS)

1.	C	6.	C	11.	D
2.	E	7.	A	12.	C
3.	B	8.	B	13.	B
4.	B	9.	C	14.	B
5.	D	10.	D	15.	C

PREPARING WRITTEN MATERIALS
EXAMINATION SECTION
TEST 1

DIRECTIONS: Each question consists of a sentence which may be classified appropriately under one of the following four categories:
    A. Incorrect because of faulty grammar or sentence structure.
    B. Incorrect because of faulty punctuation.
    C. Incorrect because of faulty spelling or capitalization.
    D. Correct

Examine each sentence carefully. Then, in the space at the right, print the capital letter preceding the option which is the BEST of the four suggested above. All incorrect sentences contain only one type of error. Consider a sentence correct if it contains none of the types of errors mentioned, although there may be other correct ways of expressing the same thought.

1. The fire apparently started in the storeroom, which is usually locked.   1.____
2. On approaching the victim two bruises were noticed by this officer.   2.____
3. The officer, who was there examined the report with great care.   3.____
4. Each employee in the office had a separate desk.   4.____
5. The suggested procedure is similar to the one now in use.   5.____
6. No one was more pleased with the new procedure than the chauffeur.   6.____
7. He tried to pursuade her to change the procedure.   7.____
8. The total of the expenses charged to petty cash were high.   8.____
9. An understanding between him and I was finally reached.   9.____
10. It was at the supervisor's request that the clerk agreed to postpone his vacation.   10.____
11. We do not believe that it is necessary for both he and the clerk to attend the conference.   11.____
12. All employees, who display perseverance, will be given adequate recognition.   12.____
13. He regrets that some of us employees are dissatisfied with our new assignments.   13.____

14. "Do you think that the raise was merited," asked the supervisor?   14._____

15. The new manual of procedure is a valuable supplament to our rules and regulation.   15._____

16. The typist admitted that she had attempted to pursuade the other employees to assist her in her work.   16._____

17. The supervisor asked that all amendments to the regulations be handled by you and I.   17._____

18. They told both he and I that the prisoner had escaped.   18._____

19. Any superior officer, who, disregards the just complaints of his subordinates, is remiss in the performance of his duty.   19._____

20. Only those members of the national organization who resided in the Middle west attended the conference in Chicago.   20._____

21. We told him to give the investigation assignment to whoever was available.   21._____

22. Please do not disappoint and embarass us by not appearing in court.   22._____

23. Despite the efforts of the Supervising mechanic, the elevator could not be started.   23._____

24. The U.S. Weather Bureau, weather record for the accident date was checked.   24._____

KEY (CORRECT ANSWERS)

1.	D	11.	A
2.	A	12.	B
3.	B	13.	D
4.	D	14.	B
5.	D	15.	C
6.	D	16.	C
7.	C	17.	A
8.	A	18.	A
9.	A	19.	B
10.	D	20.	C

21. D
22. C
23. C
24. B

TEST 2

DIRECTIONS: Each question consists of a sentence. Some of the sentences contain errors in English grammar or usage, punctuation, spelling, or capitalization. A sentence does not contain an error simply because it could be written in a different manner. Choose answer:
- A. If the sentence contains an error in English grammar or usage.
- B. if the sentence contains an error in punctuation.
- C. If the sentence contains an error in spelling or capitalization
- D. If the sentence does not contain any errors.

1. The severity of the sentence prescribed by contemporary statutes—including both the former and the revised New York Penal Laws—do not depend on what crime was intended by the offender.   1._____

2. It is generally recognized that two defects in the early law of attempt played a part in the birth of burglary: (1) immunity from prosecution for conduct short of the last act before completion of the crime, and (2) the relatively minor penalty imposed for an attempt (it being a common law misdemeanor) vis-à-vis the completed offense.   2._____

3. The first sentence of the statute is applicable to employees who enter their place of employment, invited guests, and all other persons who have an express or implied license or privilege to enter the premises.   3._____

4. Contemporary criminal codes in the United States generally divide burglary into various degrees, differentiating the categories according to place, time and other attendent circumstances.   4._____

5. The assignment was completed in record time but the payroll for it has not yet been prepaid.   5._____

6. The operator, on the other hand, is willing to learn me how to use the mimeograph.   6._____

7. She is the prettiest of the three sisters.   7._____

8. She doesn't know; if the mail has arrived.   8._____

9. The doorknob of the office door is broke.   9._____

10. Although the department's supply of scratch pads and stationery have diminished considerably, the allotment for our division has not been reduced.   10._____

11. You have not told us whom you wish to designate as your secretary.   11._____

12. Upon reading the minutes of the last meeting, the new proposal was taken up for consideration.   12._____

2 (#2)

13. Before beginning the discussion, we locked the door as a precautionery measure. 13.____

14. The supervisor remarked, "Only those clerks, who perform routine work, are permitted to take a rest period." 14.____

15. Not only will this duplicating machine make accurate copies, but it will also produce a quantity of work equal to fifteen transcribing typists. 15.____

16. "Mr. Jones," said the supervisor, "we regret our inability to grant you an extention of your leave of absence." 16.____

17. Although the employees find the work monotonous and fatigueing, they rarely complain. 17.____

18. We completed the tabulation of the receipts on time despite the fact that Miss Smith our fastest operator was absent for over a week. 18.____

19. The reaction of the employees who attended the meeting, as well as the reaction of those who did not attend, indicates clearly that the schedule is satisfactory to everyone concerned. 19.____

20. Of the two employees, the one in our office is the most efficient. 20.____

21. No one can apply or even understand, the new rules and regulations. 21.____

22. A large amount of supplies were stored in the empty office. 22.____

23. If an employee is occassionally asked to work overtime, he should do so willingly. 23.____

24. It is true that the new procedures are difficult to use but, we are certain that you will learn them quickly. 24.____

25. The office manager said that he did not know who would be given a large allotment under the new plan. 25.____

3 (#2)

KEY (CORRECT ANSWERS)

1.	A	11.	D
2.	D	12.	A
3.	D	13.	C
4.	C	14.	B
5.	C	15.	A
6.	A	16.	C
7.	D	17.	C
8.	B	18.	B
9.	A	19.	D
10.	A	20.	A

21. B
22. A
23. C
24. B
25. D

TEST 3

DIRECTIONS: Each of the following sentences may be classified MOST appropriately under one of the following categories:
  A. Faulty because of incorrect grammar
  B. Faulty because of incorrect punctuation
  C. Faulty because of incorrect capitalization
  D. Correct

Examine each sentence carefully. Then, in the space at the right, print the capital letter preceding the option which is the BEST of the four suggested above. All incorrect sentence contain but one type of error. Consider a sentence correct if it contains none of the types of errors mentioned, even though there may be other correct ways of expressing the same thought.

1. The desk, as well as the chairs, were moved out of the office. 1.____

2. The clerk whose production was greatest for the month won a day's vacation as first prize. 2.____

3. Upon entering the room, the employees were found hard at work at their desks. 3.____

4. John Smith our new employee always arrives at work on time. 4.____

5. Punish whoever is guilty of stealing the money. 5.____

6. Intelligent and persistent effort lead to success no matter what the job may be. 6.____

7. The secretary asked, "can you call again at three o'clock?" 7.____

8. He told us, that if the report was not accepted at the next meeting, it would have to be rewritten. 8.____

9. He would not have sent the letter if he had known that it would cause so much excitement. 9.____

10. We all looked forward to him coming to visit us. 10.____

11. If you find that you are unable to complete the assignment please notify me as soon as possible. 11.____

12. Every girl in the office went home on time but me; there was still some work for me to finish. 12.____

13. He wanted to know who the letter was addressed to, Mr. Brown or Mr. Smith. 13.____

14. "Mr. Jones, he said, please answer this letter as soon as possible." 14.____

15. The new clerk had an unusual accent inasmuch as he was born and educated in the south.   15.____

16. Although he is younger than her, he earns a higher salary.   16.____

17. Neither of the two administrators are going to attend the conference being held in Washington, D.C.   17.____

18. Since Miss Smith and Miss Jones have more experience than us, they have been given more responsible duties.   18.____

19. Mr. Shaw the supervisor of the stock room maintains an inventory of stationery and office supplies.   19.____

20. Inasmuch as this matter affects both you and I, we should take joint action.   20.____

21. Who do you think will be able to perform this highly technical work?   21.____

22. Of the two employees, John is considered the most competent.   22.____

23. He is not coming home on tuesday; we expect him next week.   23.____

24. Stenographers, as well as typists must be able to type rapidly and accurately.   24.____

25. Having been placed in the safe we were sure that the money would not be stolen.   25.____

KEY (CORRECT ANSWERS)

1.	A	11.	B
2.	D	12.	D
3.	A	13.	A
4.	B	14.	B
5.	D	15.	C
6.	A	16.	A
7.	C	17.	A
8.	B	18.	A
9.	D	19.	B
10.	A	20.	A

21.	D
22.	A
23.	C
24.	B
25.	A

TEST 4

DIRECTIONS: Each of the following sentences consist of four sentences lettered A, B, C, and D. One of the sentences in each group contains an error in grammar or punctuation. Indicate the INCORRECT sentence in each group. *PRINT THE LETTER OF THE CORRECT ANSWER IN THE SPACE AT THE RIGHT.*

1. A. Give the message to whoever is on duty.
   B. The teacher who's pupil won first prize presented the award.
   C. Between you and me, I don't expect the program to succeed.
   D. His running to catch the bus caused the accident.

   1._____

2. A. The process, which was patented only last year is already obsolete.
   B. His interest in science (which continues to the present) led him to convert his basement into a laboratory.
   C. He described the book as "verbose, repetitious, and bombastic".
   D. Our new director will need to possess three qualities: vision, patience, and fortitude.

   2._____

3. A. The length of ladder trucks varies considerably.
   B. The probationary fireman reported to the officer to who he was assigned.
   C. The lecturer emphasized the need for we firemen to be punctual.
   D. Neither the officers nor the members of the company knew about the new procedure.

   3._____

4. A. Ham and eggs is the specialty of the house.
   B. He is one of the students who are on probation.
   C. Do you think that either one of us have a chance to be nominated for president of the class?
   D. I assume that either he was to be in charge or you were.

   4._____

5. A. Its a long road that has no turn.
   B. To run is more tiring than to walk.
   C. We have been assigned three new reports: namely, the statistical summary, the narrative summary, and the budgetary summary.
   D. Had the first payment been made in January, the second would be due in April.

   5._____

6. A. Each employer has his own responsibilities.
   B. If a person speaks correctly, they make a good impression.
   C. Every one of the operators has had her vacation.
   D. Has anybody filed his report?

   6._____

7. A. The manager, with all his salesmen, was obliged to go.
   B. Who besides them is to sign the agreement?
   C. One report without the others is incomplete.
   D. Several clerks, as well as the proprietor, was injured.

   7._____

144

8. A. A suspension of these activities is expected.
    B. The machine is economical because first cost and upkeep are low.
    C. A knowledge of stenography and filing are required for this position.
    D. The condition in which the goods were received shows that the packing was not done properly.

9. A. There seems to be a great many reasons for disagreement.
    B. It does not seem possible that they could have failed.
    C. Have there always been too few applicants for these positions?
    D. There is no excuse for these errors.

10. A. We shall be pleased to answer your question.
    B. Shall we plan the meeting for Saturday?
    C. I will call you promptly at seven.
    D. Can I borrow your book after you have read it?

11. A. You are as capable as I.
    B. Everyone is willing to sign but him and me.
    C. As for he and his assistant, I cannot praise them too highly.
    D. Between you and me, I think he will be dismissed.

12. A. Our competitors bid above us last week.
    B. The survey which was began last year has not yet been completed.
    C. The operators had shown that they understood their instructions.
    D. We have never ridden over worse roads.

13. A. Who did they say was responsible?
    B. Whom did you suspect?
    C. Who do you suppose it was?
    D. Whom do you mean?

14. A. Of the two propositions, this is the worse.
    B. Which report do you consider the best—the one in January or the one in July?
    C. I believe this is the most practicable of the many plans submitted.
    D. He is the youngest employee in the organization.

15. A. The firm had but three orders last week.
    B. That doesn't really seem possible.
    C. After twenty years scarcely none of the old business remains.
    D. Has he done nothing about it?

KEY (CORRECT ANSWERS)

1. B
2. A
3. C
4. C
5. A
6. B
7. D
8. C
9. A
10. D
11. C
12. B
13. A
14. B
15. C